Rubén Blades

Consulting Editors

Hispanics of Achievement

Rubén Blades

Betty A. Marton

Chelsea House Publishers
New York   Philadelphia

CHELSEA HOUSE PUBLISHERS

Editor-in-Chief: Remmel Nunn
Managing Editor: Karyn Gullen Browne
Copy Chief: Mark Rifkin
Picture Editor: Adrian G. Allen
Art Director: Maria Epes
Assistant Art Director: Howard Brotman
Manufacturing Director: Gerald Levine
Systems Manager: Lindsey Ottman
Production Manager: Joseph Romano
Production Coordinator: Marie Claire Cebrián

Hispanics of Achievement
Senior Editor: John W. Selfridge

Staff for RUBÉN BLADES
Associate Editor: Philip Koslow
Editorial Assistant: Danielle Janusz
Designer: Robert Yaffe
Picture Researcher: Lisa Kirchner
Cover Illustration: Cynthia Lechan

First Printing

1 3 5 7 9 8 6 4 2

Library of Congress Cataloging-in-Publication Data
Marton, Betty A.
  Rubén Blades/Betty A. Marton
    p.   cm.—(Hispanics of achievement)
  Includes bibliographical references and index.
  Includes discography.
  Summary: A profile of the Panamanian lawyer and entertainer,
whose talents include singing, songwriting, and acting.
  ISBN 0-7910-1235-2
      0-7910-1262-X (pbk.)
  1. Blades, Rubén—Juvenile literature. 2. Singers—Panama—Biog-
raphy—Juvenile literature. [1. Blades, Rubén. 2. Singers. 3.
Panamanians—United States—Biography.] I. Title. II. Series.
ML3930.B58M4 1992   91-28598
782.42164'092—dc20   CIP
  [B]   MN AC

Table of Contents

Hispanics of Achievement   7

A Loss of Innocence   15

Root of Dreams   25

Following the Music   33

Breaking In   43

His Own Voice   55

Crossover Dreams   69

Hollywood and Beyond   81

Nothing But the Truth   93

Selected Discography and Filmography   102

Chronology   104

Further Reading   106

Index   109

Hispanics of Achievement

Oscar Arias Sánchez
Costa Rican president

Joan Baez
Mexican-American folksinger

Rubén Blades
Panamanian lawyer and entertainer

Jorge Luis Borges
Argentine writer

Juan Carlos
King of Spain

Pablo Casals
Spanish cellist and conductor

Miguel de Cervantes
Spanish writer

Cesar Chavez
Mexican-American labor leader

El Cid
Spanish military leader

Roberto Clemente
Puerto Rican baseball player

Salvador Dalí
Spanish painter

Plácido Domingo
Spanish singer

Gloria Estefan
Cuban-American singer

Gabriel García Márquez
Colombian writer

Pancho Gonzales
Mexican-American tennis player

Francisco José de Goya
Spanish painter

José Martí
Cuban revolutionary and poet

Rita Moreno
Puerto Rican singer and actress

Pablo Neruda
Chilean poet and diplomat

Antonia Novello
U.S. surgeon general

Octavio Paz
Mexican poet and critic

Javier Pérez de Cuéllar
Peruvian diplomat

Pablo Picasso
Spanish artist

Anthony Quinn
Mexican-American actor

Oscar de la Renta
Dominican fashion designer

Diego Rivera
Mexican painter

Linda Ronstadt
Mexican-American singer

Antonio López de Santa Anna
Mexican general and politician

George Santayana
Spanish philosopher and poet

Junípero Serra
Spanish missionary and explorer

Lee Trevino
Mexican-American golfer

Diego Velázquez
Spanish painter

Pancho Villa
Mexican revolutionary

CHELSEA HOUSE PUBLISHERS

INTRODUCTION

Hispanics of Achievement

Rodolfo Cardona

The Spanish language and many other elements of Spanish culture are present in the United States today and have been since the country's earliest beginnings. Some of these elements have come directly from the Iberian Peninsula; others have come indirectly, by way of Mexico, the Caribbean basin, and the countries of Central and South America.

Spanish culture has influenced America in many subtle ways, and consequently many Americans remain relatively unaware of the extent of its impact. The vast majority of them recognize the influence of Spanish culture in America, but they often do not realize the great importance and long history of that influence. This is partly because Americans have tended to judge the Hispanic influence in the United States in statistical terms rather than to look closely at the ways in which individual Hispanics have profoundly affected American culture. For this reason, it is fitting that Americans obtain more than a passing acquaintance with the origins of these Spanish cultural elements and gain an understanding of how they have been woven into the fabric of American society.

It is well documented that Spanish seafarers were the first to explore and colonize many of the early territories of what is today called the United States of America. For this reason, students of geography discover Hispanic names all over the map of the United States. For instance, the Strait of Juan de Fuca was named after the Spanish explorer who first navigated the waters of the Pacific Northwest; the names of states such as Arizona (arid zone), Montana (mountain), Florida (thus named because it was reached on Easter Sunday, which in Spanish is called the feast of Pascua Florida), and California (named after a fictitious land in one of the first and probably the most popular among the Spanish novels of chivalry, *Amadis of Gaul*) are all derived from Spanish; and there are numerous mountains, rivers, canyons, towns, and cities with Spanish names throughout the United States.

Not only explorers but many other illustrious figures in Spanish history have helped define American culture. For example, the 13th-century king of Spain, Alfonso X, also known as the Learned, may be unknown to the majority of Americans, but his work on the codification of Spanish law has greatly influenced the evolution of American law, particularly in the jurisdictions of the Southwest. For this contribution a statue of him stands in the rotunda of the Capitol in Washington, D.C. Likewise, the name Diego Rivera may be unfamiliar to most Americans, but this Mexican painter influenced many American artists whose paintings, commissioned during the Great Depression and the New Deal era of the 1930s, adorn the walls of government buildings throughout the United States. In recent years the contributions of Puerto Ricans, Mexicans, Mexican Americans (Chicanos), and Cubans in American cities such as Boston, Chicago, Los Angeles, Miami, Minneapolis, New York, and San Antonio have been enormous.

The importance of the Spanish language in this vast cultural complex cannot be overstated. Spanish, after all, is second only to English as the most widely spoken of Western languages within the United States as well as in the entire world. The popularity of the Spanish language in America has a long history.

In addition to Spanish exploration of the New World, the great Spanish literary tradition served as a vehicle for bringing the language and culture to America. Interest in Spanish literature in America began when English immigrants brought with them translations of Spanish masterpieces of the Golden Age. As early as 1683, private libraries in Philadelphia and Boston contained copies of the first picaresque novel, *Lazarillo de Tormes*, translations of Francisco de Quevedo's *Los Sueños*, and copies of the immortal epic of reality and illusion *Don Quixote*, by the great Spanish writer Miguel de Cervantes. It would not be surprising if Cotton Mather, the arch-Puritan, read *Don Quixote* in its original Spanish, if only to enrich his vocabulary in preparation for his writing *La fe del cristiano en 24 artículos de la Institución de Cristo, enviada a los españoles para que abran sus ojos* (The Christian's Faith in 24 Articles of the Institution of Christ, Sent to the Spaniards to Open Their Eyes), published in Boston in 1699.

Over the years, Spanish authors and their works have had a vast influence on American literature—from Washington Irving, John Steinbeck, and Ernest Hemingway in the novel to Henry Wadsworth Longfellow and Archibald MacLeish in poetry. Such important American writers as James Fenimore Cooper, Edgar Allan Poe, Walt Whitman, Mark Twain, and Herman Melville all owe a sizable debt to the Spanish literary tradition. Some writers, such as Willa Cather and Maxwell Anderson, who explored Spanish themes they came into contact with in the American Southwest and Mexico, were influenced less directly but no less profoundly.

Important contributions to a knowledge of Spanish culture in the United States were also made by many lesser known individuals—teachers, publishers, historians, entrepreneurs, and others—with a love for Spanish culture. One of the most significant of these contributions was made by Abiel Smith, a Harvard College graduate of the class of 1764, when he bequeathed stock worth $20,000 to Harvard for the support of a professor of French and Spanish. By 1819 this endowment had produced enough income to appoint a professor, and the philologist and humanist George Ticknor became the first holder of the Abiel Smith Chair, which was the very first endowed Chair at Harvard University. Other illustrious holders of the Smith Chair would include the poets Henry Wadsworth Longfellow and James Russell Lowell.

A highly respected teacher and scholar, Ticknor was also a collector of Spanish books, and as such he made a very special contribution to America's knowledge of Spanish culture. He was instrumental in amassing for Harvard libraries one of the first and most impressive collections of Spanish books in the United States. He also had a valuable personal collection of Spanish books and manuscripts, which he bequeathed to the Boston Public Library.

With the creation of the Abiel Smith Chair, Spanish language and literature courses became part of the curriculum at Harvard, which also went on to become the first American university to offer graduate studies in Romance languages. Other colleges and universities throughout the United States gradually followed Harvard's example, and today Spanish language and culture may be studied at most American institutions of higher learning.

No discussion of the Spanish influence in the United States, however brief, would be complete without a mention of the Spanish influence on art. Important American artists such as John Singer Sargent, James A. M. Whistler, Thomas Eakins, and Mary Cassatt all explored Spanish subjects and experimented with Spanish techniques. Virtually every serious American artist living today has studied the work of the Spanish masters as well as the great 20th-century Spanish painters Salvador Dalí, Joan Miró, and Pablo Picasso.

The most pervasive Spanish influence in America, however, has probably been in music. Compositions such as Leonard Bernstein's *West Side Story*, the Latinization of William Shakespeare's *Romeo and Juliet* set in New York's Puerto Rican quarter, and Aaron Copland's *Salon Mexico* are two obvious examples. In general, one can hear the influence of Latin rhythms—from tango to mambo, from guaracha to salsa—in virtually every form of American music.

This series of biographies, which Chelsea House has published under the general title HISPANICS OF ACHIEVEMENT, constitutes further recognition of—and a renewed effort to bring forth to the consciousness of America's young people—the contributions that Hispanic people have made not only in the United States but throughout the civilized world. The men and women who are featured in this series have attained a high level of accomplishment in their respective fields of endeavor and have made a permanent mark on American society.

The title of this series must be understood in its broadest possible sense: The term *Hispanics* is intended to include Spaniards, Spanish Americans, and individuals from many countries whose language and culture have either direct or indirect Spanish origins. The names of many of the people included in this series will be immediately familiar; others will be less recognizable. All, however, have attained recognition within their own countries, and often their fame has transcended their borders.

The series HISPANICS OF ACHIEVEMENT thus addresses the attainments and struggles of Hispanic people in the United States and seeks to tell the stories of individuals whose personal and professional lives in some way reflect the larger Hispanic experience. These stories are exemplary of what human beings can accomplish, often against daunting odds and by extraordinary personal sacrifice, where there is conviction and determination. Fray Junípero Serra, the 18th-century Spanish Franciscan missionary, is one such individual. Although in very poor health, he devoted the last 15 years of his life to the foundation of missions throughout California—then a mostly unsettled expanse of land—in an effort to bring a better life to Native Americans through the cultivation of crafts and animal husbandry. An example from recent times, the Mexican-American labor leader Cesar Chavez has battled bitter opposition and made untold personal sacrifices in his effort to help poor agricultural workers who have been exploited for decades on farms throughout the Southwest.

The talent with which each one of these men and women may have been endowed required dedication and hard work to develop and become fully realized. Many of them have enjoyed rewards for their efforts during their own lifetime, whereas others have died poor and unrecognized. For some it took a long time to achieve their goals, for others success came at an early age, and for still others the struggle continues. All of them, however, stand out as people whose lives have made a difference, whose achievements we need to recognize today and should continue to honor in the future.

Rubén Blades

Rubén Blades, photographed in 1991. Having made his mark as a singer, songwriter, actor, lawyer, and political commentator, Blades emerged during the 1980s as one of the most intriguing figures on the international cultural scene.

CHAPTER ONE

A Loss of Innocence

Church bells rang through the still, early morning air of Panama City on January 12, 1964, waking 16-year-old Rubén Blades from a heavy, dreamless sleep. As he struggled to consciousness, the familiar tolling of the bells—which always announced events that shaped the lives of Panamanians—filled him with a sense of dread.

Two days earlier, angry Panamanians had attacked dozens of buildings in Panama City, including the U.S. embassy, and fighting still raged through the streets. Twenty-one people had been killed by U.S. troops, and 500 more had been wounded. Most of the casualties were students from the University of Panama, but some were high school students like Rubén. For all he knew, some of his classmates could have been shot down by the heavily armed soldiers.

For two days, Rubén, his mother, father, grandmother, brothers, and sisters had gathered in the kitchen of their small home to hear radio reports of the violence that began in the U.S.-occupied Panama Canal Zone and spread throughout the tiny Latin American country. As they listened to the newscasters describing clashes between North Americans and Panamanians, the family stared at the brown box on the kitchen table as if that would help them understand the frightening turn of events. It was especially difficult for Rubén to accept what was happening around him. The violent confrontation had jolted him out of a delirious love affair he and many other young Panamanians had been carrying on with North American culture.

Most of the books, movies, and music that had filled Rubén's life ever since he was a child had come from the United States. By the time Rubén was a teenager, music in particular had become a passion. When he was not attending school, going to the movies with his grandmother, or reading, he was teaching himself the guitar and listening to the new rock and roll tunes on the radio.

For Rubén and his friends, rock and roll was a revelation. The songs and the rhythms spoke to them the way no other music had. They spent countless hours figuring out the chords and words to their favorite songs. They carried their guitars with them everywhere, playing under stairways and in school bathrooms, where their sounds would echo, imitating the rhythms and moves of popular acts such as Elvis Presley, Bill Haley and the Comets, Chuck Berry, and the newly discovered Beatles. When they went to the movies, they were likely to see such films as *Rock Around the Clock* and *Rock, Rock, Rock*, which featured performances by many of their favorite musicians.

When Rubén and his friends discovered Frankie Lymon and his group, the Teenagers—five black and Hispanic youths from New York City who sang like adults—they were astounded. When the group came to perform in Panama in 1963, the country went wild. The young rockers were greeted like royalty by thousands of breathless, star-struck fans, igniting Rubén's already fiery imagination. "Huge limos picked them up at the airport," he later recalled. "The police were out front, with their sirens blaring. Everybody went to see them as if they were the president of the world!"

Rubén had grown up with the ballads and dance music favored by his parents' generation. When he discovered the hard-driving electric guitar rhythms of rock and roll, he felt that the new music belonged to him alone. It gave him a sense of power and made him feel connected to the great world beyond his small country. When he sang and listened to rock and roll, anything seemed possible— until that January morning when the ringing bells made Rubén groan with the unhappy memory of the previous days' events.

The trouble had begun in the Panama Canal Zone (often referred to simply as the Zone), the 10-mile-wide, 40-mile-long

A freighter passes through the Miraflores Locks of the Panama Canal in 1961. Opened in 1914, the canal brought benefits to Panama, but it also divided the country in half and made it a virtual colony of the United States.

stretch of land in the center of the country that surrounds the Panama Canal. North American high school students, the sons and daughters of the U.S. military and civilian personnel who lived in the Zone, had raised the U.S. flag over Balboa High School without flying the Panamanian flag next to it. Their actions directly violated a 1960 agreement stipulating that both flags were to be flown together. Zone authorities promptly brought the U.S. flag down and dismissed the students' act as a youthful show of national pride. However, the students raised the flag again the next day, this time egged on by their parents. "Rather than create a situation," explained Paul Runnestrand, executive assistant to the Canal Zone governor, "we decided just to let it go."

"Letting it go" was enough of a spark to ignite half a century of resentment about U.S. involvement in Panama. When angry Panamanians marched into the Zone to protest the insult to their flag, the U.S. authorities treated the protesters like an invading army. The violence that followed shook the entire country.

In 1964, the Panama Canal was both a strategic military position and a key artery of commerce connecting the Atlantic and Pacific oceans through Central America. It was also a symbol of North American power, both in the United States and Panama. Construction of the canal had begun in 1881, when Panama, the first European settlement on the South American continent, was still part of Colombia, its larger neighbor to the east. Under the direction of Ferdinand-Marie de Lesseps, who had built the Suez Canal in Egypt, a French company began to carve a route through the middle of Panama. After some 20,000 workers had died from tropical diseases, the company went bankrupt and abandoned the project in 1887.

In 1902, the United States, seeking a short sea route between its Atlantic and Pacific coasts, purchased France's rights to develop the canal. When the government of Colombia refused to allow the project to resume, the United States encouraged the Panamanians to revolt against Colombian rule and helped them set up an independent government. President Theodore Roosevelt, the champion of U.S. expansion, offered Panama $10 million plus $250,000 annual rent for perpetual control of the canal and the narrow strip of land surrounding it.

The construction of the canal, officially opened in 1914, was a massive undertaking that cost more than $336 million. The gigantic project produced a number of benefits for Panama. In order to complete the work, U.S. engineers were obliged to modernize Panama's railroad system; at the same time, under the leadership of Colonel William C. Gorgas of the U.S. Army, public health officers made important advances in sanitation and medicine, most notably the eradication of yellow fever. However, despite the benefits that U.S. money and technology brought to Panamanians, the political reality of the canal treaty made the Republic of Panama a virtual colony of the United States.

By 1964, the fees paid by the United States for control of the canal had increased to $1.9 million annually. The number of U.S. citizens in the Zone—soldiers and civilians, along with their families—had swelled to nearly 40,000. They lived segregated from the rest of the country in a middle-class suburban paradise owned and operated by the U.S. Panama Canal Company. The Zone essentially split the country in two, and Panamanians needed permission to cross from one side of their country to the other. But the greatest rift of all, one that widened with each passing year, arose from the vast difference in the way the U.S. citizens and the Panamanians lived.

Life in the Zone was close to ideal, even by U.S. standards. There was no unemployment, no poverty, no disease. There was 1 doctor for every 350 people (compared to 1 per 750 in the United States). Most residents of the Zone lived in comfortable two-story houses surrounded by well-manicured lawns and luxuriant gardens. They had their own golf courses and beaches, air-conditioned theaters, nightclubs, and country clubs. Their children attended free schools and played in clean, well-constructed playgrounds.

This 1963 photograph illustrates the contrast between the U.S. Canal Zone and the rest of Panama. Above the chain-link fence on the left are the comfortable homes of the Canal Zone personnel; on the other side are the slums of Panama City.

The comfortable, tax-free life kept many families living in the Zone for generations. For the rest of the country, though, life was usually far different.

Less than 100 yards from the chain-link fence that marked the boundaries of the Zone, many of Panama City's 300,000 residents lived in wooden shacks, enduring hopeless poverty. In the notorious slum ironically called Hollywood, 60 percent of the people were unemployed; rats, lice, and disease were rampant; and small children played naked in unpaved streets. On the other end of Panama's social spectrum, some 20 wealthy families controlled most of the country's economic activities—breweries, newspapers, radio and television stations, sugar mills, construction firms, and other enterprises. All these lucrative businesses served the residents of the Zone, providing goods and services that few Panamanians could afford.

To most Panamanians, the Zone was a small-scale replica of the United States. It mirrored the images they saw at their local movie theaters—beautiful people with big cars and houses, bountiful good health, and unlimited opportunity. Panamanians of all ages envied this culture. Teenagers such as Rubén Blades listened hungrily to North American rock and roll music, waited for the latest word in North American fashions, and dreamed of a life that seemed to offer far more than what was possible in their small country.

The U.S. government was not entirely blind to the problems and aspirations of Panamanians. The United States provided jobs for 16,000 Panamanian citizens, and although the Panamanian government seemed to ignore the needs of its own poor, the United States helped build schools and hospitals that were superior to those in other Latin American countries. When the Panamanians' resentment of U.S. influence in their country did boil over in occasional protests and outbreaks of violence, the tension was usually defused in short order. Until that fateful day in January 1964, many Panamanian citizens seemed mollified by the agreement to fly the Panamanian flag alongside the U.S. flag within the Zone. Some took it as a sign that the North Americans were loosening their grip on the country and the canal.

After the U.S. students raised the Stars and Stripes over Balboa High School on January 9, a few dozen Panamanian students marched into the Zone to plant their flag next to it. They were promptly escorted out by Zone police, but they returned a few hours later, backed by hundreds of adults. U.S. troops responded with a barrage of bullets and tear gas. When the smoke lifted, seven Panamanian students were dead.

The citizens of Panama could not contain their fury. Enraged mobs armed with sticks, stones, and homemade firebombs clashed

Panamanian students marching in November 1964, behind a banner that reads The Canal Is Ours. Panamanians' anger at U.S. domination of their country had boiled over at the beginning of 1964, leading to battles between demonstrators and U.S. troops.

with U.S. troops. Inside the Zone, the four-story U.S. Information Agency building was destroyed. Fires were set at buildings owned by U.S. airlines and rubber companies. The next day, the rioting flowed over onto the streets of Panama City. More American businesses and government buildings, including the U.S. embassy, were attacked, their windows smashed with rocks. After 2 days of fighting, 21 Panamanians and 3 American soldiers were dead; 500 Panamanians were wounded, and another 250 were in jail.

For young Rubén Blades, the world would never again be the same. His image of the United States as a kindhearted giant dispensing fantastic music and movies was gone forever. He turned his back on rock and roll and immersed himself in the history and the music of his culture. He began playing with local Afro-Cuban bands and writing songs far different from the rock and roll tunes he had previously loved. Instead of focusing on the trials and tribulations of young love, Rubén's songs dealt with the lives and struggles of the people around him. Equally important, he now refused to sing in English.

"I couldn't believe what happened," Blades said many years later. "Until then the North Americans were always the good guys. We knew that from the movies, didn't we? They were the guys we'd seen kicking the Nazis, beating the bad guys. And all of a sudden, you had them on the other side shooting at you! It was a big disappointment. And a lot of us started asking hard questions, not taking everything so literally anymore. I began to read a lot more history, politics. There was a tremendous loss of innocence." For Rubén Blades, that loss of innocence was also a coming of age.

Frankie Lymon, the 14-year-old lead singer of the group Frankie Lymon and the Teenagers, rehearses during a tour of Great Britain in 1957. When Blades was in high school, he idolized Lymon and dreamed in vain of joining the Teenagers.

CHAPTER TWO

Root of Dreams

Rubén Blades, Jr., was born in Panama City on July 16, 1948. He was the second of five children in a family of musicians and artists. His father, Rubén, Sr., was a policeman and also a musician who played the bongos, a pair of small drums often featured in Latin music. Rubén's mother, Anoland, was the daughter of a Cuban mother and a U.S. citizen who had fought in Cuba with Theodore Roosevelt's Rough Riders during the Spanish-American War in 1898. Before moving from Cuba to Panama, Anoland sang with Ernesto Lecuona, one of Cuba's greatest songwriters. She also played the piano and worked as an actress on radio *novelas*, or soap operas. She had first met Rubén Blades, Sr., when she was singing with a band in which he played the bongos.

Young Rubén's family background mirrored the racial and cultural diversity of Panama itself. His paternal grandfather, who worked as an accountant, had come to Panama from St. Lucia, a British colony in the West Indies. After marrying Rubén's Colombian-born grandmother, Emma Bosques Laurenza, and

fathering several children, he suddenly disappeared, leaving Emma
to raise the family. She proved more than equal to the task.

Emma Bosques Laurenza had a profound influence on her
grandson Rubén. Throughout her life, she had shown an unusually
independent spirit. As a young girl, she completed high school,
which was the highest education available in Panama at the time.
She practiced yoga and was a member of the Rosicrucians, an
international fraternity of religious mystics. Grandmother Emma
believed so deeply in her spiritual powers that she claimed the
ability to move objects without touching them, a process known as
telekinesis. She was also a feminist; because she had struggled
to survive in what she viewed as a "man's world," she sent her
daughters to school and educated her sons at home. She was also a
vegetarian, a writer, and a painter. When he was older, Blades
described his grandmother Emma as "a wonderfully crazy woman
who instilled in me the silly notion that justice is important and that
we can all serve and be part of the solution."

Young Rubén spent most of his time with his grandmother. His
parents were not often home because, he recalled, they "never
stopped working. They always wanted [the children] to be ahead
of them." Using comic books, Grandmother Emma taught Rubén
to read when he was four years old. She also introduced him to
modern art and took him regularly to American movies to escape
the oppressive heat of the Panamanian summer. The family's tiny
apartment on Calle Segunda (Second Street) did not even contain
ceiling fans; when the *abanicos*, little hand fans, failed to disperse
the hot air, Rubén and his grandmother would pay 15 cents apiece
for seats in the Teatro Edison, the neighborhood movie house.

"It had the coldest refrigeration system I have ever been in—in
Panama, in New York, in Europe, anywhere on earth!" Blades
recalled. "That place was cold, man. You had to bring a jacket; there
were penguins in the aisles! So we used to go every afternoon and
watch movies all day. And they always used to show us, for reasons
unknown to me, newsreels from Europe. You'd have the music in

Trombonist Glenn Miller and his orchestra performing in 1940, when they were great favorites in Panama. When Blades was growing up, his generation turned away from Miller's big-band sound and embraced rock and roll. "The older people had their dance, now we had ours," he said.

the back: 'And the chancellor of Germany, Herr So-and-so, has just . . .' You know, in this theater filled with Panamanians trying to escape the heat!"

By the time he began attending school, Rubén was also becoming more aware of music. "We were a radio family," he recalled. "In those days, you had a lot of time on your hands, so we would sit down wherever we could sit down in the house and listen to the radio. We would listen to guys like Beny Moré, of course, or the Orquesta Casino de la Playa. But in Panama they would also play Mel Tormé, Nat King Cole, Glenn Miller and Harry James. Duke Ellington, too. The disc jockeys—it was anarchic, they just played what they wanted to hear, so you'd get everything from the Blue Tango to Pérez Prado."

When Rubén was six, Beny Moré came to Panama. Rubén and his family, along with everyone else in the neighborhood, went to see Moré perform with his group. The experience made a lasting impression on the young boy. Riding high above the dancing crowd on his father's shoulders, Rubén was astonished by what he saw and heard. The stage was filled with musicians dressed in brilliant white suits. Golden horns flashed as the musicians swayed with the energy of the sounds they created. The dancers—blacks,

whites, and mulattoes (those of mixed black and white ancestry)—
were stirred to a frenzy by the energy of the musicians who were
having as much, if not more, fun than their appreciative audience.
At one point, Rubén's father got him close enough so he could
actually touch Beny Moré's hand. It was a thrill Rubén never forgot.
"It was really something to see these Latin musicians, proud as hell,
having a great time in their sharp-looking suits," he recalled. "But
still, I was looking at people who were like my father. It didn't
matter that Beny Moré was only 26 at the time. I looked at him and
saw my father."

By 1956, however, the rock and roll music that had taken
over young people in the United States and England had reached
Panama, and the Spanish-speaking radio stations began to broadcast the new English-language songs. It made no difference to
Rubén that he could not understand the lyrics. The music said it all.

"Rock and roll was a real turning point for all the young guys
down there," said Blades. "We didn't understand the words, but
there was some kind of thing in there. Something we could intu-
itively associate, I guess, with what we were: kids. Regardless of
where they're from, kids are kids. . . . We saw kids singing like adults
[in the movies], and we said, 'Wait a minute, we can do this, too.'
Frankie Lymon was 14 years old; you looked at him and you knew
it was a kid, not an old man. And also, rock and roll came with a
dance. The boleros and all that stuff, that was an older type of
dance, very formal, a grown-up type of dance. But rock and roll was
just running around and going under someone's legs and doing
whatever you felt like doing and having a nice time. The older
people had their dance, now we had ours."

When Frankie Lymon and the Teenagers came to Panama
like conquering heroes, Rubén was there among the throngs that
greeted them. He knew by heart every song the group performed,
and he felt that his own singing talents qualified him to be the sixth
Teenager. He wrote Frankie Lymon a letter asking for an audition
and gave it to his mother to mail. He was furious when he found out

Elvis Presley gyrates during a performance in the 1950s. When Blades's mother threw away the letter her son wrote to Frankie Lymon asking for an audition, she made amends by buying Rubén a plastic guitar with an image of Presley, another of his favorites.

that she threw the letter away. Rubén's mother had other ideas for his future. But she made it up to him by buying him a plastic guitar with a decal of Elvis Presley and a hound dog, commemorating Presley's hit record "Hound Dog."

When the first Beatles tunes were released in Panama in 1963, Rubén was immediately entranced. Here was another group of teenagers who had formed a band, developed their own music, and played in small clubs until they finally got the chance to cut a record. Now they were on their way to fame and fortune. A week after the Beatles' 1964 debut on "The Ed Sullivan Show" in New York, Rubén saw the program on the Southern Command Network, broadcast from the Canal Zone.

"I keep trying to explain this to North Americans," he said years later. "They think about Panama as some foreign place where people don't know what's going on. But we got them all, Gene Vincent, the Platters, Jackie Wilson, Billy Stewart. We were just as much a part of the rock and roll movement as young people in the States. And that was true everywhere."

Rubén's constant practicing with his friends paid off in his first public performance in 1963, when he was 15. One night, his brother Luis's band, the Saints, were performing in competition with a band known as the Monsters, and Luis asked Rubén to sing. Despite his mother's protests, Rubén agreed, and his singing was a hit with the audience. After that, he performed regularly with the Saints, singing covers of Frank Sinatra and other North American pop and rock favorites.

"My mother never wanted me to go in the band, because they got paid for the gigs, maybe three, four dollars, which was a fortune in those days," Blades recalled. "She was always afraid of what I might do if I had money. Money meant mobility."

Many adults associated rock and roll music with wild and dangerous behavior, but in Rubén's case, his mother's fears were unnecessary. He had other interests in addition to music and other outlets for his restless energy. Ever since his grandmother taught him to read he had taken an avid interest in books. As a teenager, he read constantly and was especially fond of novels of fantasy and adventure, such as Robert Louis Stevenson's *Treasure Island*. He often dreamed of going off to live in some enchanted place, perhaps the South Seas depicted in Stevenson's tale of pirates and buried treasure.

The Beatles, photographed during a 1966 TV performance. The four young rockers from the working-class section of Liverpool, England, were special heroes for Blades and his friends: They had formed a band when still in their teens and had played small clubs before achieving stardom.

Because of his vivid imagination and lively curiosity, Rubén also reacted to the poverty and injustice that existed in Panama. Although he admired the culture of the United States, he also began to understand that Panama's neighbor to the north was hardly a perfect society. The same television channels that featured "The Ed Sullivan Show" and suburban sitcoms such as "Father Knows Best" also carried newsreels showing black civil rights demonstrators being attacked by police dogs in the South. Finally, in January 1964, when American students refused to fly the Panamanian flag and 21 Panamanian protesters were killed by U.S. troops, Rubén's infatuation with North American culture came to a painful end. "I stopped and looked at myself and realized that I was a Panamanian, and that my eyes weren't going to turn blue," he recalled. "I realized that I had to deal with the reality of who I am."

Rubén turned away from rock and roll and began to channel his enthusiasm into Latin music. He came to love the street energy and the elegance of Joe Cuba, the Puerto Rican *típica* sound (based on folk music) of Cortijo y Su Combo, and the music of Ismael and Mon Rivera. He was also taken with an Argentine singer named Piero. Instead of the traditional Latin love ballads, Piero sang about social themes and issues and about what life was really like in the neighborhood and the city. Rubén felt an instinctive pull toward the deeply moving messages in Piero's music.

When the Argentine balladeer came to play in Panama, Rubén, carrying his guitar, went with a friend to meet Piero at his hotel. Rubén had written a song called "Pablo Pueblo," and he thought that if he played it for Piero, the Argentine might want to record it. Piero agreed to hear the song and listened thoughtfully as Rubén strummed and sang.

When Rubén was finished, Piero said abruptly, "I can't record this." Rubén's face, always expressive, showed his deep disappointment.

"Why not?" Rubén asked.

"Because it's a good song and I want you to record it," Piero replied. "That way there will be two of us."

The Arcadia Ballroom in 1954. Located in the heart of New York City's Times Square, the Arcadia was the first downtown night spot in New York to feature Latin music.

CHAPTER THREE

Following the Music

After the 1964 riots, Panama's volatile political scene took a positive turn. President Marco A. Robles, who had been narrowly elected shortly after the riots, opened negotiations with the United States in the hope of revising the 1903 canal treaty. Although the negotiations did not succeed, they began a process that bore fruit in 1977, when the United States finally agreed to place the canal under Panamanian control in the year 2000. Perhaps more important, Robles attempted to correct some of the nation's glaring economic inequities by reforming the tax laws and creating opportunities for the disadvantaged. To foreign observers, Robles appeared capable of being the first leader to create a real nation out of Panama.

In reality, the Robles government never enjoyed strong support at home, and the president's efforts at economic reform stirred up powerful opposition. In the 1968 elections, the voters turned to Arnulfo Arias, a fiery right-winger whose career history reflected the instability of Panamanian politics.

Arias had been elected president in 1940 and was ousted by a coup a year later. He ran for the presidency again in 1948, lost the election, and then led a successful coup of his own the following year. After jailing his enemies and ruling as a virtual dictator, he was deposed once more in 1951. Following his election to a third term in 1968, Arias made a desperate effort to protect himself against another military coup. He tried to replace the National Guard, Panama's elite military corps, with a new unit whose loyalty he could count on. Reacting swiftly, however, the officers of the National Guard mobilized their forces and turned Arias out of office only 11 days after he had assumed power.

Seeing the idealistic Robles give way to the dictator Arias, the 20-year-old Blades was deeply concerned about Panama's political future. At the same time, his parents were urging him to develop a career that would be more stable than that of a musician. As a result, he enrolled in the University of Panama to study law. However, he continued to write music and, when he had time, to perform with Afro-Cuban bands. When he cut an album with a group called Bush and the Magnificos, his singing attracted the attention of a New York producer named Pancho Cristal. Cristal contacted Blades and offered him the chance to replace Cheo Feliciano, who was leaving Joe Cuba's band. It was a tempting opportunity, the kind of break that Blades had often dreamed about, but he also felt deeply committed to his studies. Hoping it would not be his last chance at performing with a topflight band, Blades turned down Cristal's offer.

As a college student in the late 1960s, Rubén was already an astute political observer. The impressions he gathered formed the basis of a 1985 article published in New York's *Village Voice*. Describing Arias and the 1968 coup that ended his third term as president, Blades's article reveals much about Panamanian politics and the people's disillusionment with its political leaders.

People voted for Arnulfo because he was Arnulfo. Period. He had created Panama's National Security Institution. He had been an Axis sympathizer [a supporter of Germany and Japan] during World War II. He gave women the right to vote. He was a notorious racist who could not stand blacks or Asians. He was the only Panamanian doctor ever to graduate from Harvard. He was the only Panamanian doctor who refused to lend his services during the 1964 Canal Zone riots, when General O'Meara's Southern Command Forces were shooting down Panamanians of all ages and the country needed every available medic to tend its wounded... In spite of the contradictions, Arnulfo always came out on top of the political polls. In 1968 he prepared to take the country on another of his dramatic rides. No one seemed to care about the possiblility of faulty brakes; . . . people tired of being cheated by less colorful politicians never found the Arias experience a boring one. So he led them to his social roller coaster and they followed suit.

On the night in 1968 when Arias was overthrown, Rubén planned to go out with a classmate named Zozimo. They were going to

Arnulfo Arias, shown addressing a Panamanian court in 1951, served three tumultuous terms as president of Panama. The turmoil following Arias's 1968 ouster from office interrupted Blades's college studies. As a result, Blades had a chance to explore the Latin music scene in New York.

play dominoes and have some beers at a club called Fuerza y Luz (Power and Light). As he was showering, his mother asked him where he was going. "Out," he said, hoping to end the conversation.

"My mother, informed of my whereabouts, invariably showed up to check on her son's activities, convinced that in doing so she was saving me from a life of crime," Blades recalled. "Although I was a law student at the time, my mother was certain that my true vocation was to become a full-time hoodlum; school was just my way of trying to fool her and the rest of the good citizens of Panama."

Although Anoland Blades may have underestimated her son's common sense, she had a remarkable knack for making predictions. That evening she told Rubén that a military coup was under way in the Chiriquí province, near the border of Costa Rica. Nothing of the sort had been reported in the news, and Rubén interpreted the tale as his mother's last-ditch attempt to make him stay at home.

"After asking if she would be gracious enough to loan me a couple of dollars—which I promised to repay after my first big heist—I agreed to take a portable radio and listen to the news. If there was anything suspicious, I would get back home immediately. Reluctantly, she took out two crumpled dollar bills and, before handing them to me, she asked where I was going. I told her we were going to a party at a nearby barrio [neighborhood] called Bethania. 'You are lying,' she said solemnly. I took the radio, signed a receipt for it, gave her a kiss on the forehead and left the house, feeling my mother's eyes on me all the way to the street where Zozimo's horrendous purple car waited for the push that would take us to the Fuerza y Luz and to the final and absolute vindication of my mother's psychic powers."

The coup by the National Guard eventually led to widespread agricultural, economic, and social reform programs instituted by the guard's commander, Colonel Omar Torrijos Herrera. But before Torrijos revealed his intentions, progressive Panamanians regarded him as merely another brutal dictator. Upon taking over the government in October, Torrijos immediately dissolved the National Assembly and created a new governing body that proclaimed him Panama's "maximum chief." During the November 3 Independence Day celebration, 1,000 students and faculty members from the University of Panama protested Torrijos's actions. Armed troops attacked the protesters, and more than 200 of them were hauled off to jail. In order to stifle further dissent, the government closed down the university and arrested a number of student leaders. Blades was not arrested, but the government's action had a far-reaching effect on his life.

With the university shut down, Blades was at loose ends. He recalled the offer he had received not long before to cut a record with Joe Cuba's band. With help from his brother Luis, who was working for an airline, he bought a discount ticket and took off for New York.

Arriving in New York City in 1969, Blades walked into the middle of a less violent but equally profound upheaval. The num-

Machito and His Orchestra, photographed in 1945. During the 1940s, musicians such as Machito and Tito Puente defined the Latin sound in the United States, providing arrangements of traditional Cuban, Puerto Rican, and Dominican dance forms.

ber of Puerto Ricans, Mexicans, Cubans, Dominicans, and others of Latin American descent living in the United States had increased by 40 percent during the 1960s. With this increase in numbers came a growth in pride and self-awareness. As black civil rights activists, antiwar protesters, gays, and other groups expressed their ideas and aspirations, Hispanics also began to understand that they had common problems that called for concerted action. The first step for Latins living in the big cities was a new sense of pride, beginning with a celebration of their language and their rich heritage of literature, art, music, and dance.

The musical expression of the Latin revolution came to be known as salsa. The word *salsa*, which means "sauce" in Spanish— specifically a spicy sauce of tomatoes, onions, and hot peppers—is a convenient label for the fast-paced, rhythmic beat of the urban barrios. The music itself, on the other hand, is not so easy to define. According to Tony Sabournin, a Latin-music critic from New York, salsa is "90 percent Afro-Cuban music with 10 percent Puerto Rican influences, unless you talk to someone from Puerto Rico. Then it's the other way around."

Students of music tend to agree with both statements. Charley Gerard and Marty Sheller, in their book *Salsa! The Rhythm of Latin Music*, emphasize that the roots of salsa are definitely Cuban. Historically, the island of Cuba was a hotbed of Latin music; there the traditional music of the Spanish colonists meshed with the vital folk rhythms of the many African slaves who were imported to work on the sugar plantations. During the 20th century, Afro-Cuban music, as it came to be known, was taken up by Puerto Ricans living in New York City, who referred to themselves as Nuyoricans. The Nuyorican musicians seized upon traditional Afro-Cuban forms such as the tango, the rumba, and the bugalú and combined them with elements of North American jazz, rock, and rhythm and blues. The result was salsa.

The New York nightclub scene provided the perfect setting for this kind of musical cross-fertilization. During the 1940s and 1950s, audiences had flocked to Broadway dance halls such as the Pal-

Saxophonist Charlie Parker and trumpeter Dizzy Gillespie (center) are flanked by bassist Tommy Potter and saxophonist John Coltrane during a 1951 session at New York's Birdland. Parker and Gillespie often jammed with Latin musicians and helped create the new musical form known as salsa.

ladium and the Arcadia, dancing the tango, the rumba, and the samba to the elegant music of such Latin greats as Tito Puente and Machito. Birdland, the famous jazz club, was only a few steps away; when jazz titans such as Charlie Parker and Dizzy Gillespie wound up their sets they would often join the Latin musicians onstage, improvising a sound that was new to all. Out of these sessions grew such phenomena as Gillespie's Cubop, the first Latin-influenced jazz movement, and the jazzing up of Latin dance music that eventually produced the salsa sound.

By the time Blades arrived in New York, the salsa revolution was in full swing. Like the other movements of the day, salsa belonged to young people who gathered nightly at places such as the Cheetah Club on 53rd Street between Eighth and Ninth Avenues. There 18-year-old Hector LaVoe sang regularly with Willie Colón's two-trombone band. In contrast with the more established musicians—suave, well-dressed Johnny Pacheco or gentle, conga-playing Ray Barretto—Willie, Hector, and their group flaunted the swagger and toughness of their Puerto Rican neighborhood in the Bronx. "Eighty percent of their dances ended in fights, that's what we loved about them," explained Tony Sabournin.

Blades was ready for salsa in all its varieties, smooth or rough. But he felt that it could be taken further. The music with the irresistible beat could carry lyrics that went far beyond "Mira, mira, baby let's dance." Blades believed there should be songs that addressed the barrio, the city, the country, the whole continent, songs that grappled with the way people lived their lives.

Many standard lyrics made Blades laugh with their old-fashioned, romantic irrelevance. "I used to hear the bands play an old song, which typically went: 'On the golden hill, the rooster wakes you up,'" Blades remembered in a 1987 *New York Times* interview. "I thought, hey, wait a minute. Most of these people never set foot on a mountain. And it's not a rooster that wakes them up, but a G.E. alarm clock."

Willie Colón and his band were among the leaders of the salsa movement when Blades made his first visit to New York in 1968. After hearing all the performers on the salsa circuit, Blades decided that he had a contribution to make.

As soon as he found a place to stay, Blades contacted Pancho Cristal, the producer who had offered him a chance with Joe Cuba's band. Cristal hooked him up with Pete Rodríguez, who had heard Blades sing in Panama. Together they cut *De Panamá a Nueva York* (From Panama to New York), an album on which Blades wrote the lyrics for all but one of the songs. Performing with one of the top Latin artists of the day, Blades believed that he was beginning a major music career. But bugalú, the sound for which Rodríguez was famous, was a dying fad, and the album never sold. After a few months, Blades learned that back in Panama the National Guard had relented and reopened the university. He decided to return home and finish his degree.

In 1972, Blades graduated from the University of Panama, took a job as an attorney for the Banco Nacional de Panamá, and spent much of his spare time counseling prisoners. His parents were pleased that he was settling into a solid career, and he himself felt that he was doing important work. But before long he began to feel dissatisfied. He had never lost his passion for music, and he continued to perform with local bands and write his own songs. In addition, he had had a taste of New York City and wanted more. He began to feel that he could reach more people with his political ideas as a singer and songwriter than he could as a lawyer. Perhaps most important, he was wrestling with a deep personal need that only music could satisfy.

"I think artists become artists because they're seeking some kind of love or affection," he later explained. "There's some kind of insecurity that can only be alleviated or resolved through approval from an external source. I think I became a singer because there was something lacking in my emotional life."

In 1974, after two years of working as a lawyer, Blades decided to follow his deepest instincts. He quit his job, packed his bags, and headed back to New York City.

Rubén Blades and Willie Colón with disc jockey Symphony Sid at New York's Village Gate. The combination of Blades's songs and Colón's musical arrangements created a revolution in the salsa movement.

CHAPTER FOUR

Breaking In

When Blades arrived again in Manhattan, he took a job as a law clerk with the Panamanian consulate. His parents were pleased; the position appeared to be the first step of a career in the Panamanian foreign service. Blades himself was still drawn toward the idea of being a lawyer, because it offered him a means of putting his political ideas into practice. However, he did not forget for a moment that he had come back to New York in order to explore the music scene. He began by devoting all his spare time to music, but he soon found that being only a part-time musician would not enable him to realize his musical ambitions.

Blades wanted to push Latin music beyond its customary themes—a man being betrayed by his best friend; a man leaving a woman; a woman's broken heart mending only to be broken again. He wanted to sing about other issues that affected the heart, soul, and life of Latin Americans.

His years at the University of Panama had given Blades a deeper understanding of political issues. The disciplined study of history and political science had focused the sense of justice he had absorbed from his grandmother and the outrage he had felt when seeing political corruption and oppression, both in Panama and in New York. He began to write songs about the raw reality of the city streets, about the lives of people he knew in Panama, and about the Latin barrios in New York City.

Blades was not by any means the first songwriter who tried to confront social issues through music. Piero, the Argentine musician he had so admired as a high school student, wrote many songs about social issues. So did the West Indian calypso singers—Lord Cobra, Lord Delicious, and the Mighty Sparrow—whom Blades had heard during his youth in Panama. As early as the 1920s, the German poet Bertolt Brecht had joined forces with composer Kurt Weill to create *The Threepenny Opera*, a biting attack on the conditions that produce crime and poverty. During the tumultuous 1960s, North American singer-songwriters such as Pete Seeger, Bob Dylan, Joan Baez, Tom Paxton, and Buffy Saint-Marie had achieved popular acclaim with songs of protest against exploitation, racism, and war.

Joan Baez (center) and Bob Dylan perform with Joni Mitchell (left) at Madison Square Garden in 1975. Dylan and Baez had both become stars while singing political protest songs; taking his cue from their success, Blades believed that he could convey his own message through the salsa beat.

Blades did not see any salsa musicians following this path. He felt that salsa musicians did not realize the impact they had on their audiences, nor did they understand what life in Latin America was all about. Blades believed that music was a way for poor Hispanics, in both the United States and Latin America, to reach beyond the confines of the barrio and realize that their problems and their struggles were shared by peoples throughout the world.

When Blades was offered a post in the Panamanian embassy in Washington, D.C., he had to choose between a career in the foreign service and the highly unstable life of a musician. He decided to give up his secure position and hit the streets with his six-string guitar, beginning an endless round of auditions for New York club owners and record companies. He tried to convince them of the need to produce an urban folklore that people could identify with, not just through rhythmic patterns but through subject matter. But those who controlled the Latin music world resisted. They realized that the young Panamanian musician was someone to watch, but they were not ready to take a chance on his political ideas; they were afraid that his songs would never catch on with the keyed-up salsa audiences.

As Blades recalled, "They looked at my songs and said, 'These songs are too long. Where's the hook? And there are too many lyrics and the people aren't interested in this, they just want to dance.' So I prepared myself to accept rejection. Not from an emotional point of view, because I was so sure what I was doing was correct, but from a practical point of view. I had to survive. And rejection can cause economic problems. So I took a job. I saved my money. That's the only way to save the integrity of your work and yourself."

Blades signed on for $73 a week as a mail-room clerk at Fania Records, a leading producer and distributor of salsa music. If his own music was not being recorded, Blades reasoned, he at least wanted to be associated with music that was. He made the rounds of the New York salsa scene almost nightly, stopping in such nightclubs as the Cheetah, the Cork & Bottle, Casa Blanca, El Corso, and the Red Garter. There he heard musicians such as Willie Colón, Ray Barretto, Larry Harlow, and Johnny Pacheco perform. Excellent as these musicians were, they were not addressing the issues that in Blades's mind most affected the lives of their listeners. He was convinced more than ever that he had a contribution to make.

Sleeping on the floor of his small studio apartment on a mattress he had found in the street, Blades knew he would be living very differently if he had taken the embassy job. Despite his sense of mission, he did not enjoy the role of a poor immigrant, and he knew that his mother, who thought that every germ in the world was ready to jump on anything that fell on the floor, would be horrified by his way of life.

He spent hours walking the streets of New York, scribbling lyrics to new songs on the brown paper bags left over from his takeout meals. When a new melody popped into his head, he would rush home like a man possessed, whistling the tune over and over so he would not forget it, and then work out the notes on his guitar. Songs would also come to him as he was pushing crates of records and bins of mail along 57th Street. Collecting his meager paycheck, he hoped that his break would come before he got too discouraged.

Blades's first big break came when he appeared with drummer Ray Barretto and his band at Madison Square Garden in 1974. Blades was extremely nervous during the concert, but the audience liked him, and Barretto offered the young singer a permanent job.

A few months after he began to work at Fania, Blades was contacted by bandleader and percussionist Ray Barretto. Adalberto Santiago, one of Barretto's powerful vocalists, was leaving to form his own group, Típica 73, and Barretto's lead singer, Tito Gómez, needed someone to back him up. Barretto had heard Blades sing and felt that he might fill the bill.

Blades made his debut with Ray Barretto at Madison Square Garden in April 1974. Thrust into the world of big-time conventional salsa with little preparation, Blades was extremely nervous and missed several cues onstage. But the audience responded to his rich baritone voice as well as his boyish good looks and the macho swagger he could adopt when it suited him.

Blades earned himself a spot with Barretto's band and got his first taste of touring. He was thrilled to learn that audiences throughout the world, not only in Latin America but in Europe and Asia as well, loved the hot salsa sound. Having established himself with Barretto, Blades also performed with the Fania All-Stars, a group of Fania's best-known musicians who toured nationally and internationally. When the Fania All-Stars performed at Yankee Stadium, 40,000 fans responded rapturously. People rushed onto the field at the end of the show to be near the musicians, some even climbing down from the upper deck via the netting behind home plate.

Blades learned a great deal while performing with Barretto and the Fania All-Stars, but he was not satisfied to remain at this level. He was only one salsa singer among many, and he was not reaching enough people—certainly not the poor and illiterate Latins in barrios in the United States and abroad with whom Blades longed to connect. Music was his only chance to communicate with these people. He was sure that they would appreciate the message of the songs he was writing—if only they had the chance to hear them.

The executives at Fania kept the creativity of their musicians on a short leash in order to cater to the conservative international market. Many artists found this policy stifling. Ray Barretto was among them; shortly after Blades joined his group, Barretto left Fania for the more progressive jazz scene. After his departure, the remaining members of his group formed a new group called Guarare, and Blades performed with them for nearly two years.

Although salsa producers were reluctant to give Blades a chance to perform his own compositions, other musicians had their eye on the young songwriter. While Blades was with Guarare, Bobby Rodríguez and Ismael Miranda made hit recordings of two of his compositions, "El Tren Número Seis" (The #6 Train) and "Cipriano Armenteros," a tale of a 19th-century Latin American outlaw. The recordings got the attention of Jerry Masucci, Fania's founder. Masucci had been watching Blades closely. When he saw that other performers were having success with Blades's material, he asked Willie Colón if he was interested in working with Blades.

Colón, a Bronx-born trombonist, was a star on the salsa circuit. For 10 years he had been playing with Hector LaVoe. During that time he had proved to be an original talent. Colón introduced rhythmic elements of Puerto Rican folk music, such as *bomba* and *plena*, into the basic Cuban and Puerto Rican salsa tunes; he also imbued his music with Jamaican, Brazilian, and other influences. Colón was attracted to the melodic structures of Blades's songs, and by 1976 he was ready to move away from the hard-driving LaVoe. Recognizing this, Jerry Masucci decided it was time to take a chance on Blades. Colón's willingness to work with Blades, whose talents veered away from the tried-and-true salsa mode, would be a mark of distinction for the newcomer.

The collaboration of Colón and Blades turned out to be a fruitful one, both for themselves and for Fania. Although their first album, *Metiendo Mano* (Butting In), was received with only moderate enthusiasm, they went on to make salsa history with their next album, *Siembra* (Planting). Blades wrote seven of the eight songs on *Siembra*, addressing such social issues as racial prejudice and the foolishness of people whose main values are fashion and style.

Blades (second row, center) poses with Cuban-born vocalist Celia Cruz and other members of the Fania All-Stars in 1975. The All-Stars, selected from the musicians under contract to Fania Records, performed to rapturous audiences throughout the Americas.

All the songs became immensely popular, but the cut "Pedro Navaja" was the biggest hit. For that song, Blades borrowed both lyrically and musically from the sinister Brecht-Weill ballad "Die Moritat von Mackie Messer" (successfully recorded in a slicked-up English version as "Mack the Knife" by both Frank Sinatra and Bobby Darin). "Pedro Navaja" tells the dark, mysterious story of a barrio murder. Its narrative power and social lesson were a big departure from traditional salsa, and it offered a welcome change just when many salsa fans were beginning to turn toward disco. "Pedro Navaja" has since become Blades's signature tune, a song that his fans call out for at every concert.

With *Siembra*, Blades and Colón also brought salsa to the attention of Latin audiences who had previously ignored it. Such countries as Argentina, Spain, and Mexico had never cultivated salsa music, and university-educated Latin Americans did not tend to be salsa fans. Although political songwriting, called *nueva canción* (new song), had long been popular with politically aware young people in Latin America, it was missing something that Blades and Colón supplied—a catchy beat. Combining Colón's unique and powerful arrangements with Blades's word-pictures, *Siembra* created new salsa fans in Puerto Rico and New York, Panama and Venezuela, Colombia and Mexico, and even Spain. The album was Fania's first million seller, selling more than 3 million copies worldwide.

Despite *Siembra*'s success, Fania was not ready to support Blades's wider ambitions. Blades, who had grown up in a society where diverse races, cultures, and languages existed side by side, was not willing to limit his appeal to a purely Latin audience. He wanted to reach out to Anglo-Americans as well and teach them about the social and political issues affecting the lives of Latin people. But the executives who ran Fania and other Latin-oriented record companies found it hard to believe that their non-Latin audiences would accept anything but the stereotyped version of Latin music that went with ruffled shirts, maracas, and "Besame Mucho," a highly popular romantic ballad. Nevertheless, because Colón and Blades were making money, Fania did not interfere with them.

In 1980, Blades wrote "Tiburón" (Shark) to express his feelings about American and Soviet interference in the internal political affairs of other nations. At the time, the cold war between the United States and the Soviet Union was still a serious issue. Ever since the Cuban revolution of 1959, the Soviets had supported Cuba's Communist government. At the same time, the United States had done everything it could to prevent the spread of communism in Latin America, going so far as to engineer the 1973 overthrow of Salvador Allende, Chile's freely elected left-wing president. Six years later, the Soviets began a brutal war in Afghanistan, trying to set up a Communist government in that Asian nation. Blades's song equally condemns both superpowers, using the image of the shark to depict the way they prey upon smaller nations:

> The moon rests amidst the silence
> Resting on the great Caribbean
> Only the shark is still awake
> Only the shark is on the prowl
> Only the shark is still restless.

Despite its balanced viewpoint, "Tiburón" created a furor in Miami's Little Havana, a neighborhood populated mostly by Cubans who had fled their homeland after the revolution. These exiles were so fiercely anti-Communist that any criticism of the United States struck them as Communist propaganda. As a result, Miami's most popular Latin radio station broadcast an editorial labeling Blades a Communist and banned "Tiburón" from its playlist. The controversy upset Blades's parents, who had moved to Miami, and resulted in several death threats against the songwriter. Blades took the threats seriously enough to buy himself a bulletproof vest before setting foot in Miami, and he decided it was best not to perform there. He wanted to shrug off his Cuban critics, but he was deeply stung by their failure to understand what he was saying.

"Some Cubans in Miami have a very peculiar view of dictatorship," he explained. "They talk about political prisoners in Cuba but not in Chile. They would applaud an invasion of Nicaragua [then governed by a left-wing regime] but remained conspicuously silent for years about [Anastasio] Somoza [the brutal Nicaraguan dictator overthrown by the leftists]. They complain about the repressive regime in Cuba, but they ban my records!"

Despite his growing success as a musician, Blades constantly sought new challenges. In 1981, he played a boxer in the low-budget film The Last Fight; *the film was a disaster, but Blades found that he enjoyed being an actor.*

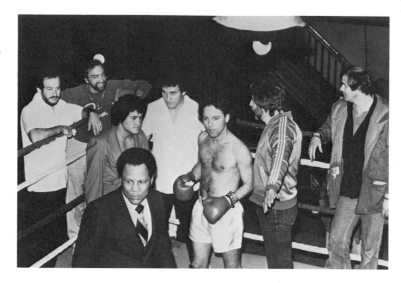

Outside Miami, "Tiburón" did nothing to diminish the growing popularity of Blades and his music. Blades and Colón toured often throughout Europe, the Caribbean, and South America. They played regularly to capacity audiences at nightclubs in New York, Washington, D.C., and Los Angeles. But before long, even songwriting was too narrow a focus for Blades's ambitions. When he was not tied up rehearsing or performing, he began to write short stories and essays and published a column in the Panamanian newspaper *Estrella de Panamá* (Panamanian Star).

As he had done as a child, Blades continued to read voraciously, often rereading his favorite authors. He had rented a modest apartment on Columbus Avenue on the Upper West Side of Manhattan, and although he could afford to live much better than he had as a mail-room clerk, he limited his furniture to the basic necessities. Even his stereo system was a simple one for someone who made his living as a musician. Blades's main possessions were books; yards of them lined the walls. On his bookshelves, 20th-century classics by Ernest Hemingway, William Faulkner, Anaïs Nin, and Albert Camus shared space with contemporary writers such as Fran Leibowitz, Woody Allen, Octavio Paz, and Gabriel García Márquez.

Much to his excitement, Blades began to correspond with García Márquez, the Nobel Prize–winning Colombian novelist who attempted to capture the essence of the Latin American experience in his often mystical tales of love and politics. Blades was impressed to learn that the literary García Márquez was also a salsa fan and that his skills as a writer were enhanced by his understanding and appreciation of popular culture.

Blades's 1980 album, *Maestra Vida* (Life the Teacher), was the first among his works to be directly inspired by García Márquez. Produced by Fania in two parts, again in collaboration with Willie Colón, *Maestra Vida* is actually an opera about three generations of a Latin American family of urban laborers. Although this unusual format appealed to relatively few listeners, the album demonstrated the breadth of Blades's narrative powers.

Clearly, Blades owed his commercial and artistic success to his collaboration with Willie Colón. After nearly six years, however, the partnership was beginning to confine both men. After they completed another album in 1982, it was becoming apparent that Blades and Colón needed to travel in different directions. Specifically, Blades was ready to differentiate himself from Colón's brass-oriented sound and develop a truly individual style. Having broken into the world of salsa, he was ready to break out.

Blades poses on the steps of a New York tenement, in a photo for the cover of his Escenas *album. Blades's agreement with Elektra/Asylum made him the first Latin artist under contract to a major label for albums in both Spanish and English.*

CHAPTER FIVE

His Own Voice

When Rubén Blades broke with Willie Colón in 1982, he carefully recruited the musicians who could help fulfill his vision of salsa music—Oscar Hernández on piano and electric guitar, Mike Viñas on electric and acoustic guitars and chorus, Louie Rivera on bongos and percussion, and Ralph Irizarry on timbales (kettledrums) and percussion. Most significant, he replaced Colón's traditional horn section with Ricardo Marrero's vibraphones, producing a tighter, smoother sound that allowed more focus on the lyrics.

The name of Blades's new group, Seis del Solar (Six from the Tenement), clearly suggested a grass-roots approach, but the music itself indicated that Blades was reaching far beyond the so-called *cuchifrito* circuit. (Cuchifritos are a form of deep-fried fast food popular in Puerto Rican neighborhoods.) In order to broaden his appeal to Anglo-American and international audiences, which did not take easily to traditional salsa, Blades began to incorporate some of the rock and jazz sounds that had appealed to him as

55

Blades with the members of Seis del Solar, the band he formed in 1982. Blades's new arrangements kept the traditional salsa beat but achieved a unique sound by using vibraphones in the place of trumpets and trombones.

a teenager. By using more elegant keyboard arrangements and Marrero's vibes, he hoped to capture the interest of a more diverse audience.

Blades's effort to blur the lines between salsa and mainstream North American music continued to cause conflicts with Fania Records. In addition to his creative differences with the company's management, Blades discovered that Fania had been shortchanging him. For example, although the *Siembra* album had sold 3 million copies worldwide, Blades had received only $15,000 in royalties. Exploitation of performers and songwriters was an old story in the music business, but Blades was not prepared to become another victim. With the benefit of his legal training, he filed suit against Fania. As a result, he got back the copyrights to all his songs and won the right to larger royalties from his future record sales.

Once he had obtained justice, Blades broke with Fania completely. In 1984, he became the first Latin artist to sign with

Elektra/Asylum Records, a division of Warner Communications and one of the leading mainstream labels.

Blades was not the first *salsero* to try to cross over with a major-label contract, but he was the first under contract for both Spanish and English albums with the same prominent recording company. Elektra's executives compared him favorably with such artists as folk-rocker Bob Dylan and Jamaican reggae singer Bob Marley, both of whom had achieved stardom with music that carried a strong social message. However, Blades did not take his deal with Elektra as a sure ticket to fame and fortune. Rather, he viewed his move into the mainstream as an opportunity to communicate with a wider audience. With this in mind, he insisted that his own English translations be included with each of his Spanish albums, and vice versa.

Jamaican reggae star Bob Marley, photographed during a 1978 concert. Marley's politically charged music, his international reputation, and his status as a national hero in Jamaica made him a powerful inspiration to Blades.

BUSCANDO AMÉRICA

Estoy buscando a América y temo no encontrarla.
Sus huellas se han perdido entre la oscuridad.
Estoy llamando a América pero no me responde.
Le han desaparecido los que temen la verdad.

Envueltos entre sombras, negamos lo que es cierto:
mientras no haya justicia, jamás tendremos paz.
Viviendo dictaduras, te busco y no te encuentro.
Tu torturado cuerpo no saben dónde está.

Te han secuestrado América, y amordazado tu boca,
y a nosotros nos toca ponerte en libertad.
Te estoy llamando, América. Nuestro futuro espera.
Antes que se nos muera, ayúdenme a buscar.

Coro:
Te Estoy buscando América,
te estoy llamando América.

SEARCHING FOR AMERICA

I'm searching for America, and I fear I won't find it.
Its traces have become lost amongst the darkness.
I'm calling for America but it can't answer me.
Those afraid of truth have made her disappear.

Surrounded by shadows we deny the certain;
(while we live) without justice there will never be peace.
Living under dictatorships I search but I can't find you;
no one knows where your tortured body is.

You have been kidnapped, America; you have been
gagged, and it is up to us to free you.
I'm calling for you, America. Our future awaits;
before it dies, help me to search.

Chorus:
I'm searching for America,
I'm calling for America.

In signing with Elektra, however, Blades faced hurdles that had
tripped up many artists who had tried to go beyond the success they
had achieved with a limited audience. More often than not the
switch to English and the adoption of rock and other mainstream
styles tended to dilute the power of the original sound. Blades was
aware of the challenge and discussed it candidly in a 1984 interview
with Robert Palmer of the *New York Times*.

"The basic elements in any successful crossover would have to
be honesty and quality," Blades told Palmer. "I would never want to
lose my audience by trying to present a salad of an album, with one
or two songs in English, to appeal to whom exactly? I'll always keep
the basics of the music, the Afro-Cuban structure, the language. But
I'll give the music little twists; I've never subscribed to the idea that
the music will disappear if you change it a bit. When I signed with
Elektra, my ambition wasn't to make a crossover album. I wanted to
make an urban American album that can be appreciated by any
American city dweller and might bring people who haven't identified with salsa a bit closer to us."

Buscando América (Searching for America), Blades's first album
with Elektra, sold more than 400,000 copies, 300,000 within the first
5 months. The album was nominated for a Grammy Award and
made several top 10 lists for pop albums in 1984. No salsa recording
had ever before achieved such a distinction. Music critic Jay Cocks,
writing in *Time* magazine, asserted, "If there is a better album this
year in any language, its impact will have to be measured off the
charts. On the Richter scale, maybe." (The Richter scale is used by
scientists to measure the force of earthquakes.) The album also
scored high grades in publications as diverse as *Rolling Stone* and
the *Village Voice*.

Although *Buscando América* attracted more non-Latin fans than
any salsa record had before, many traditional salsa fans could not
decide what to make of the album. Blades still respected the basic
3/2 beat of salsa, called *clave* (KLAH-vay) because it is usually laid
down with a pair of round sticks known as *claves*. He also kept the

traditional chorus in his songs, following what Gerard and Sheller decribe as "the call-and-response pattern [between lead singer and backup] which typifies many of the African-derived musics of the New World." At the same time, Blades borrowed liberally from rock and jazz to achieve what he called a more "urban sound."

On balance, Blades insisted that when it came to the emotional content of the music, "The passion is Latin." "I couldn't just take away the Afro-Cuban format," he explained. "It was the only link to the people. I basically kept the music and changed the lyrics."

Blades's lyrics were evolving into a form of political protest against conditions in Latin America. With political ferment on the rise, dictators and their henchmen systematically murdered known opposition leaders, civilians suspected of disloyalty, and even religious and humanitarian workers—including priests and nuns—whose activities threatened the government.

Events in Panama were especially disturbing to Blades. The reforms heralded by Colonel Omar Torrijos in 1968 were soon short-circuited by a shortage of funds, by corruption, by drug trafficking, and by a host of other internal and external political problems. By the early 1980s, employment and productivity had declined even in the Panama Canal Zone. The lack of progress in negotiations with the United States to ensure Panama's control of the canal only added to the tiny nation's woes.

In 1981, when General Torrijos's private plane crashed in the Panamanian mountains, General Manuel Antonio Noriega, who controlled a violent wing of the National Guard, rose to power. Noriega, who for years had worked closely with the U.S. Central Intelligence Agency, controlled a lucrative drug trade. As the virtual dictator of Panama, he continued to fill his own pockets at the expense of the country.

Blades maintained close ties to Panama, visiting his homeland two or three times a year. He was outraged by the poverty and the human rights violations he witnessed in Panama and elsewhere in Latin America. In addition to expressing his feelings in music, he

General Manuel Antonio Noriega took control of the Panamanian government in 1981. The advent of Noriega, a notorious drug trafficker who ran a brutal and corrupt regime, motivated Blades to plan a positive role for himself in the political future of Panama.

also began to speak publicly about his desire to eventually run for political office in Panama.

In *Buscando América*, Blades made his political statements through intimate portraits of individuals trying to survive in desperate circumstances. He was especially gratified that the album sold 200,000 copies in Latin America. It meant that his message was reaching people not only in the United States but throughout the Western Hemisphere.

One of the principal songs on the album was inspired by the murder of Archbishop Oscar Arnulfo Romero in El Salvador, one of Panama's neighbors in Central America. Archbishop Romero, who had often criticized the Salvadoran government for its abuse of human rights, was gunned down in March 1980, right on the altar of the San Salvador Cathedral. His death aroused international outrage and led to the eruption of a long and lethal civil war in El Salvador. When news of the murder reached Blades in New York, he felt that evil had finally triumphed over good. He knew that the only way he could ever come to terms with his feelings was to express his outrage in his music.

The resulting song was entitled "El Padre Antonio y el Monaguillo Andrés" (Father Antonio and the Altar Boy, Andrés). Blades worked on the song over a period of nine months, carefully developing the main characters. Father Antonio is an idealistic priest who has left his post at the Vatican in Rome because he has no taste for "paper work and air conditioned dreams" and has gone to the jungles of Latin America to work with the poor. Andrés is a happy-go-lucky 10 year old who loves to skip school so he can wander along the river and play soccer. His family hopes that the Catholic church, in the person of Father Antonio, will help straighten Andrés out. At the conclusion, when the priest is assassinated on the altar, Andrés dies alongside him:

Archbishop Oscar Arnulfo Romero of El Salvador, an outspoken defender of human rights, was gunned down by an assassin in 1980. This brutal act inspired Blades to write one of his most powerful protest songs, "El Padre Antonio y el Monaguillo Andrés."

Antonio fell, host in hand and, without knowing why,
Andrés fell beside him, never having met Pelé;
surrounded by surprise and the screaming,
once more agonizing
was the wooden effigy of Christ, nailed to the wall.
The identity of the criminal was never known.
The bells ring one, two, three times
for Father Antonio and his altar boy, Andrés.

"GDBD," short for Gente Despertando Bajo Dictatura (People Awakening Under Dictatorship), one of Blades's favorite cuts from the album, originally came to life as a short story before Blades reworked it and set it to music. The song follows the movements of a seemingly ordinary man as he wakes up on an ordinary workday and stumbles unhappily through his washing, dressing, and breakfast routines. Depicting the petty annoyances that almost everyone endures, the song creates a certain sympathy for the main character—until he gets a call from his office, giving him his instructions for the day. Then he collects his notebook, his dark glasses, and his gun, puts on his jacket, and goes out to arrest someone. The ordinary working man turns out to be a secret policeman, routinely doing the dirty work for the dictators of Latin America.

For the benefit of anyone who might wonder what the policeman's job entails, Blades spells it out in the next song on the album, "Desapariciones" (Disappearances). Here Blades expresses the fear and anxiety of four people whose loved ones have just vanished, as if into thin air—a common experience in countries such as Nicaragua, El Salvador, Chile, and Argentina, where the secret police have at times arrested thousands of people simply on suspicion of opposing the government. The lucky ones are beaten, tortured, and released; most are killed, their bodies thrown into mass graves. As described by Blades, this is the daily reality for many Latin Americans:

Last night I heard several explosions.
Shots from rifles and revolvers.
Speeding cars, brakes screeching, screams.
The echo of boots in the street.
The noise of banging at doors. Complaints.
Oh my god's. Broken dishes.
They were showing the soap opera on the TV.
No one looked outside.

When he was writing music, Blades incorporated all sorts of diverse materials. In "Padre Antonio," for example, he re-created the sound of the church bells he had heard from his bedroom in

Relatives of political prisoners demonstrate in Buenos Aires, Argentina, in 1982. The atrocities committed by right-wing regimes were a frightening daily reality for many people in Latin America; Blades dramatized this desperate situation in songs such as "GDBD" and "Desapariciones."

Panama City; the bells resound throughout the song as a symbol of hope. In New York, on his way to recording sessions, he was enthralled by a musical sculpture that stood in the middle of Times Square, at Broadway and 46th Street. During the day, it was impossible to hear anything above the traffic noise. But in the still of the night, the wind made the sculpture emit a long, drawn-out, high-pitched humming sound. Blades went out at three o'clock one morning to tape the sound. Later in the studio, he played it back and started humming whatever melody came into his mind. Then he asked the members of his band to play some street riffs and blended the new melody into the barrio beat.

Blades's approach to songwriting was equally off the cuff. "I have a drawer with little bits of paper," he explained to an interviewer. "Once in a while, I look at them, and if there's that burst of enthusiasm, I know it's time to do the song; it's like they hatch themselves. When I have enough good ones, I call the guys and say, 'Okay, write the charts and let's go into the studio.'"

After the release of *Buscando América,* Seis del Solar embarked on a concert tour that included Berkeley, California; the Cannes Film Festival in France; and New York City. During the summer of 1984, the group performed at the prestigious Montreux International Jazz Festival in Switzerland before touring Puerto Rico, Colombia, Ecuador, and Panama.

In Panama, however, *Buscando América* met with official opposition. Panama's government censorship committee objected in particular to the song "Decisiones" (Decisions), a series of character sketches that includes a young woman who fears she may be pregnant as she awaits her menstrual period. The authorities insisted that the song promoted abortion and refused to allow Seis del Solar to perform it in Panama. Despite this act of censorship, Blades's music reached the people he cared about. The controversy over the censorship was aired in the newspapers for 2 weeks; tapes of "Decisiones" were played all over the country, even on buses; and

20,000 people, the largest crowd ever assembled for a nonpolitical event in Panama, came to hear Seis del Solar perform in concert.

After the *Buscando América* tour, Blades began work on several new projects, including the soundtrack for *Beat Street,* a movie about break dancing, and a long-distance collaboration with Gabriel García Márquez on a cycle of songs based on the writer's stories.

Before these efforts were completed, Blades received word that his application to Harvard University for a master's degree in international law had been accepted. The intensive one-year program would take him out of the limelight to Cambridge, Massachusetts, and help prepare him for a political career, which he already envisioned as including a campaign for the presidency of Panama.

Some of Blades's fans were upset by this news, both because Blades was stepping away from his music career and because he would be attending a university closely identified with the North American power structure. Blades defended his decision as a way of building his credentials. "I am totally convinced that I am going to have a lot to do with the future of my country," he declared. "But I don't want people to say, 'What does this guy know? He's been singing.'"

Rubén Blades performs in the film Crossover Dreams. *During the early 1980s, Blades began traveling in many directions at once; his ventures into new fields won him many fans but also drew criticism from former associates.*

CHAPTER SIX

Crossover Dreams

Blades's move to Cambridge in the fall of 1984 was at first oddly reminiscent of his early days in New York City a decade before. Once again, he was a stranger in a strange land. But unlike Manhattan, Cambridge was a long way from the salsa circuit. Separated from downtown Boston by the Charles River and dominated by Harvard University, much of Cambridge retains the atmosphere of a 19th-century New England town. For someone accustomed to New York's fast pace and heady ethnic and cultural mixture, the genteel, Anglo-Saxon environment of Harvard required a major adjustment.

The drastic change of surroundings, along with a feeling of solitude that followed the end of his romance with New York songwriter Lisa Carlson, sent Blades into a depression during his first few months at Harvard. He was so down that he barely took the trouble to stay in touch with old friends. It had been years since he was a student, tackling abstract legal theory and case studies, and the work load was enormous. But the academic en-

vironment also provided him with an opportunity to exercise his
mental powers and discuss world affairs with some of the outstand-
ing legal scholars in the country.

After years of playing late nights in clubs and touring with a
hard-living crowd, Blades now rarely touched alcohol and had all
but quit smoking cigarettes. Hitting the books for long hours in his
studio apartment, he would allow himself only an occasional glass
of sherry and would indulge in a cigarette only when he had to sit
up far into the night.

As Blades began to get his bearings in Cambridge, he allowed
himself more of a social life. Cambridge may have been a tradition-
ally Anglo-Saxon community, but there were quite a few Latins
studying and teaching at Harvard. Occasionally, Blades would join
some graduate students and younger faculty members for an evening. They would sit around eating rice and beans, drinking rum,
listening to salsa, dancing and singing, telling jokes, and arguing
politics. Sometimes Blades would bring his guitar and offer a few
samples from the album he was soon to record.

Although far from Manhattan and focused in a new direction,
Blades was still involved with several projects he had started before
beginning school. The most important of these, a film called *Crossover Dreams*, thrust Blades into the limelight as an actor. Since his
early days, when he sat in the frigid Teatro Edison with his grandmother Emma in order to escape the oppressive Panamanian heat,
Blades had been mesmerized by the silver screen, and he wanted to
try his hand at acting.

His first opportunity to break into film came in 1981. Seeking
to capitalize on the success of Colón and Blades's album *Siembra*,
Jerry Masucci of Fania wanted to make a film about a boxer's life,
to be called *The Last Fight*. Masucci hired Fred "the Hammer"
Williamson, a former football player turned actor, to direct. From
the start, Blades sensed that the film would flop: The makeshift
production team, from writers to producers, was not really professional, and the end result was terrible. Although the entire process

A view of Widener Library in Harvard Yard. Blades's move to Harvard University was a drastic and difficult transition, but he felt that he needed a graduate law degree to increase his political standing in Panama.

had left a bad taste in Blades's mouth, he was still aching to act. When he saw a 1979 film called *El Super,* which was highly acclaimed for its sensitive portrayal of the Hispanic community in the United States, he got in touch with the producers, Max Mambru Films.

Manuel Arce and Octavio Soler of Max Mambru had already met Blades just before he made *The Last Fight.* At that time they were producing a series of short films for the late-night comedy show "Saturday Night Live." Blades, whom they admired as the "shooting star" of salsa, had a brief cameo appearance in one skit. When he told Arce and Soler that he was interested in making a full-length film, they were intrigued.

Arce was working on a script with director Leon Ichaso about a salsa singer who leaves behind his girlfriend, his friends, and the barrio for a chance to make it big in mainstream circles. Although Blades had had no professional training as an actor, he was an instinctive performer. When Arce and Ichaso got a taste of Blades's natural and laid-back style of acting, they offered him the role of the central character, Rudy Veloz. Recognizing Blades's writing ability and his knowledge of the music industry, the filmmakers also gave him the opportunity to help shape the script.

Before they began shooting in August 1982, Arce and Ichaso spent long evenings with Blades in his Columbus Avenue apartment, refining the character of Rudy Veloz, the salsero who betrays his past for the chance to move beyond the cuchifrito circuit. The character of Rudy Veloz was one Blades knew intimately. His experience of the temptations and pitfalls that Latin musicians face helped create the story of *Crossover Dreams*. Blades also wrote and recorded "Good for Baby," the song that momentarily catapults Rudy Veloz out of the barrio.

In an interview in *Rolling Stone* magazine, Blades described the message of the film this way: "What we were saying was success and happiness are not achieved by crossing over. Your life is not going to be any easier. You just bring your problems with you."

Creating *Crossover Dreams* turned out to be a long, difficult but rewarding experience. As independent filmmakers, Max Mambru operated on a shoestring budget. They shot *Crossover Dreams* mostly in New York's East Harlem barrio, relying on the cooperation—and often the generosity—of the people who lived in the neighborhood. Film crews painted neighborhood apartments in return for being allowed to film in them, and residents often cooked meals for the hardworking crew. The actors and the rest of the company agreed to a Screen Actors Guild contract that deferred most of their salaries until after the completion of the film, and the actors' wardrobes were made up mostly of their own clothes. In one unfortunate incident, the van in which the clothes were kept was stolen one night from a public parking lot across from the studio's offices. Among the items taken was a leather jacket Blades had worn in several scenes. In order to continue the filming, Blades had to replace the jacket with his own money.

The tight budget slowed down production of the film. The producers often had to postpone editing and reshooting certain scenes, and it was two years before the film was ready for distribution. At one point Max Mambru turned to German television,

Blades poses with the cast and crew of Crossover Dreams. *Although the film received good reviews, the production process was a long, hard struggle: Lack of money often caused a halt in the filming, and Blades took time off to pursue other projects.*

which bought the film as a work in progress, paying the producers just enough to cover expenses and finish the movie.

During the many months the film was being reworked, Blades had moved on to other projects: He had signed with Elektra and was recording *Buscando América.* Then he went on tour and began to study at Harvard. The more time passed, the more he resisted breaking away from his new projects to reshoot scenes and help promote *Crossover Dreams.* When he finally did show up to shoot the final scenes, he had shaved off the mustache he had worn throughout the beginning of the film and had to wear a fake one.

Blades's attitude angered some of those who were working so hard to wrap up the movie and get it distributed. Director Leon Ichaso was particularly upset with Blades and accused him of turning his back on his heritage the same way Rudy Veloz did in the movie. "He's let everyone down," Ichaso told an interviewer.

Blades was undaunted by such criticism and denied that he was a carbon copy of Rudy Veloz. "I never believed in crossover," he told an interviewer. "I believe in convergence. Instead of crossing over to the other side, at the risk of abandoning what you already have and finding no one's there waiting for you, what I propose is 'Let's meet in the middle.' For instance, on *Buscando América*, I translated the lyrics into English. That makes it possible for whoever doesn't speak Spanish to meet us halfway—as opposed to my trying to do it in English, which would have alienated all my Spanish supporters."

Crossover Dreams finally opened in March 1985 as part of the New Directors/New Films series at the Museum of Modern Art in New York City. Vincent Canby, a film critic for the *New York Times*, described Blades as "a fine new film personality, a musical performer who's also a screen natural, the kind of actor whose presence and intelligence register without apparent effort." Canby called the film a "sagely funny comedy, both heartfelt and sophisticated, a movie that may well realize the crossover dreams that elude Rudy."

Although *Crossover Dreams* was never as widely distributed as Blades, Arce, and the others had hoped, it brought Blades a wider recognition with mainstream audiences. Even before the film opened officially on August 23, 1985, at New York's Cinema Studio, Hollywood had begun to regard Blades as an important new actor. While still at Harvard, he was asked to consider at least a dozen new film scripts, including a part on the popular television series "Miami Vice."

Blades was excited by the recognition of his acting talent and thought about moving to Hollywood when he was finished at Harvard. However, he was disgusted by the kinds of roles he was being offered. He angrily turned down the chance to appear on "Miami Vice" when he discovered that they wanted him to play a drug dealer. The other possibilities were all the same. "I must have seen fifteen scripts in the last six months," he complained. "In half, they want me to play a Colombian coke dealer. In the other half, they want me to play a Cuban coke dealer. Doesn't anyone want me to play a *lawyer?*"

Refusing to portray Latin stereotypes, Blades put his acting plans on hold. As the academic year at Harvard drew to a close, he concentrated on completing his thesis. The thesis explored the relationship between the concepts of law and politics, tracing the development of these ideas from ancient Greece through the writings of contemporary Latin American authors. At the conclusion, Blades related the ideas he had discussed to the future development of Panama. It was clear to his professors that he had ambitions beyond film and music.

Blades's thesis won acceptance, and on June 6, with his mother in attendance, Blades proudly joined more than 4,500 undergraduates and graduate students in Harvard's commencement ceremonies. The event proved to be quite atypical of Harvard's starchy reputation and very much in keeping with Blades's sympathies. The ceremonies were punctuated by protests against the university's investments in South Africa: Many of the gowned graduates carried black and white balloons in reference to South Africa's oppression of blacks; other students surrounded a dormitory where a visiting South African diplomat was staying and refused to let him out. Among those receiving honorary degrees were the American sculptor Louise Nevelson and the British author V. S. Pritchett—both 85 years old and still hard at work—and Paul Volcker, the strapping, cigar-smoking chairman of the U.S. Federal Reserve Board. Accepting his degree, Volcker expressed ideas close to Blades's heart when he called for the United States to increase its aid to smaller nations and urged the graduates to devote themselves to public service. Blades certainly intended to put his master's degree to good use.

Proud at having met what he considered one of the toughest challenges of his career, Blades immediately turned his attention to

Director Leon Ichaso, shown here on the set of Crossover Dreams, *was annoyed by Blades's frequent absences and charged that the singer had turned his back on the Latin community. Blades countered that he was simply trying to bring Latin culture to a wider audience.*

recording his second album for Elektra, *Escenas* (Scenes), which featured a duet in Spanish with Linda Ronstadt and a solo on synthesizers by Joe Jackson.

With *Escenas*, for which he later won a Grammy Award, Blades stepped even further away from traditional salsa by relying more on keyboards and synthesizers. The result is a much less aggressive sound that blends surprisingly well with the quick salsa beat and Blades's unusual and poetic lyrics.

The new album also differed from *Buscando América* by concentrating more on the personal than on the political. Of the seven long cuts that make up the album, only two deal head-on with politics. "La Canción del Final del Mundo" (The Song of the End of the World) is a clear-eyed prediction of nuclear destruction in which Blades reminds his audience, "For good or for bad, we sent for it; now the bill has been handed to us and it has to be paid." In "Muévete" (Move On), Blades issues a rousing appeal for people all over the world to join the fight against injustice:

> From the Caribbean to Soweto in Africa, our song goes
> saluting those who defend freedom and use truth as a
> shield. There's not a bullet that can kill truth when reason

defends it. Let us join together to finish off evil, Move and
put your heart in it. . . . Get a move on Colombia, Méjico,
Argentina. Cuba, Guatemala, listen Costa Rica, Perú and
Nicaragua, which today needs you. Brasil and Bolivia; Chile
and Paraguay, ay! sing it Venezuela, sing it El Uruguay;
come on Jamaica, Trinidad-Tobago, come on Salvador,
let's go Martinique, Guadalupe, República Dominicana,
come on Ecuador.

For the most part, however, *Escenas* deals with emotional issues and
dark fantasies. The opening song, "Cuentas del Alma" (Heart
Dues), depicts a woman trying to fall asleep in front of the television set; ever since her husband left home, she has been afraid of
the dark. Although the singer calls the woman "my mother," it is
not clear whether Blades is writing about his own family or simply
describing the unhappiness that invades many marriages. "Now
that I'm older," he writes, "I can understand her horror; how
painful it is to love an illusion buried in the shadow of the past, that
frees itself at night and runs to her side like the ghost of a love that
never died."

This melancholy mood continues in "Tierra Dura" (Hard
Land), in which a lover's pain is expressed as a trip through a
barren, sweltering desert. However, the album's second-longest cut,
"Sorpresas" (Surprises), tells the macabre tale of a mugger who is
stabbed by a supposedly dead man whose pockets he is going
through: "And from the neighborhood to the moon his laugh
shone—'Life is full of surprises, friend.' Chorus: What do these
novices think? This is my 'barrio,' pal."

The opportunity to work with a mainstream pop star such as
Linda Ronstadt was a special treat for Blades. Ronstadt called the
experience of recording Blades's song "Silencios" (Silences) as
"singing with kisses in her voice." Sung as a duet, "Silencios" tells
the story of two unhappy lovers who stubbornly cling to their
hopeless relationship because of the fear that "we will never find
another love."

The singer Linda Ronstadt performed a duet in Spanish with Blades on the Escenas *album. Ronstadt, whose father was Mexican, had previously sung only in English; six years after* Escenas, *she won a Grammy Award for a Spanish-language album of her own,* Canciones de Mi Padre.

Writing about the personal passions revealed in *Escenas,* Pamela Bloom, a critic for *High Fidelity* magazine, said, "Let's face it, Rubén is angry. He's pushing his voice, once a rich baritone, to its tenor edge to express something more than prettiness. It's almost as if his assimilation has demanded this uncompromising self-analysis."

In yet another attempt to analyze Blades's music, one critic referred to Ronstadt's performance in Spanish as a sort of "reverse crossover." Blades saw nothing peculiar in Ronstadt singing in Spanish: Her father was Mexican, and she had grown up singing in Spanish as well as English. To his annoyance, he found that he was increasingly having to defend his intentions against other people's desire to pigeonhole musicians and their work. He was somewhat vindicated six years later when Ronstadt won the Grammy Award for Best Latin Album for *Canciones de Mi Padre* (Songs of My

Father), a record rich in her family's Mexican heritage and sung completely in Spanish.

"I want to integrate music to end this nonsense, this racist fallback," he said. "Black-music radio, white-music radio, Latin-music radio—it's another form of racism. When they try to get a certain audience, they are ultimately excluding people. Music is not exclusive, it's inclusive."

Pete Hamill, writing in *New York* magazine, confirmed Blades's ability to attract fans from all walks of life. Describing Blades's performance at New York's Village Gate during the summer of 1985, Hamill described the enthusiastic audience as consisting of "whites, blacks, Latins, Asians, young men and old, in ice-cream suits or designer jeans or punky pegged pants, college girls, older women, veterans of the original Palladium (the midtown palace of Latin music in the 1950s), women with baroque piles of hand-tended hair or brusque downtown chops, tight glittery sheaths or summer cutoffs, stiletto heels or tennis shoes." This heady mix of styles and cultures was exactly what Blades had in mind when he suggested in an interview, "Let's meet in the middle someplace, and then we'll walk together."

In the fall of 1985, as *Escenas* began to reach music stores, Blades was preparing for his October 26 debut at New York City's Carnegie Hall. Playing Carnegie Hall is the classic symbol of achievement for any performing artist; for Blades, it would also be an unmistakable sign that mainstream audiences were receiving his musical message. Although he had given dozens of concerts over the previous 11 years, appearing before huge audiences at Madison Square Garden and Latin American stadiums, he was nervous about his Carnegie Hall debut. He looked forward to October 26 with the feeling that he still had something to prove.

Blades poses for a publicity photo during the late 1980s. After renting an apartment in Los Angeles in 1987, Blades took on a number of film roles; although the films often failed at the box office, his performances were praised by critics.

CHAPTER SEVEN

Hollywood and Beyond

Looking down from the stage of Carnegie Hall, Rubén Blades opened his concert by thanking the audience for attending—first in Spanish and then in English. It was a relief, after all his anticipation, to actually be standing in front of what had turned out to be a sold-out auditorium. Although he could hardly make out individual faces from the stage, Blades knew he was performing for the kind of integrated audience that he had worked so hard to attract. He was playing not just for die-hard salsa fans or even Latin-music followers but for a group that, in the words of a reviewer from the *Village Voice*, "closely resembled a United Nations delegates' lounge."

Blades made sure the audience experienced the full spectrum of his music and his ideas. For non-Spanish speakers, he introduced and summarized the theme of each song in English. "I am talking so much tonight because we don't have enough forums to express ideas," he explained. He went on to speak about such topics as racism, the political roots of the terrible famine gripping the African nation of Ethiopia, and the reasons why his song "Decisiones" was banned in Panama. He introduced "La Canción del Final del Mundo," his warning of imminent nuclear destruction, by wryly suggesting that everyone get up and dance.

Seis del Solar, with a bassist, twin keyboards, and four percussionists, held the attention of the audience all evening. After ending the set with a *guaguanco* (pronounced hwa-HWAN-co), a version of the street rhythms heard in Latin barrios throughout the Western Hemisphere, Blades and the musicians left the stage to a standing ovation. "Carnegie Hall represents the mainstream United States culture that Mr. Blades wants to reach," wrote reviewer Jon Pareles in the *New York Times,* "and he is doing so, triumphantly, on his own terms."

Following the concert, Blades resumed his New York routine. He was happy to be back in the city after his year at Harvard. Even though his Columbus Avenue neighborhood had begun to change, with pricey boutiques replacing the familiar shops and bodegas (small groceries), Blades was still energized by the city, and he immediately launched into a string of projects and appearances.

Shortly after the concert, he spent an afternoon in Washington Square Park with Lou Reed, Bruce Springsteen, Bono of U2, and other popular rock musicians, making "Sun City," a music video produced by Steve Van Zandt, a former member of Springsteen's E Street Band, to protest the repressive racial policies of the South African government. The video was part of a larger project, which included an album, a long-form video, and a benefit concert, all done under the collective name Artists United Against Apartheid.

Blades was excited to join forces with other performers who were also concerned about politics. He took the opportunity to ask Springsteen, whom he admired for returning rock and roll to the kind of social commentary it had lacked since the heyday of Bob Dylan, how he felt when people failed to understand the meaning behind his music.

Blades strolls along New York's Sixth Avenue in 1985. Although the ethnic flavor of his old neighborhood was tainted by gentrification during the 1980s, Blades continued to derive inspiration from New York City's lively street life and cultural diversity.

"Once you finish a song, once you've written it and recorded it and made the statement, you really don't have any control over it any more," Springsteen replied. "The most you can do is be very clear all the time about what you do and where you're going and not be influenced by anything else."

Springsteen's attitude echoed Blades's own feelings and helped, once again, to reaffirm the necessity behind his work. "The bottom line," Blades said, "is that you never know how a song will affect anyone else. . . . You just make the statement and hope that it will be understood and that it'll do some good at some point."

Although he was generally idealistic, Blades always emphasized the hard realities to any young songwriter who asked his advice:

> The first thing I ask, out of my experience, is, "Did you register your song?" If not, I tell him how to do it. . . . I might show him how to fix a line or a word. I tell him over and over: It's a long trip, it's a long trip. I tell them not to think about an easy success, you know, write a song, have a hit, sell a million. If that's what you're thinking you might as well write comic books or soap operas. You have to write because you have something to say. And I tell them to read. Read as much as they can. I tell them I'm still learning to write every day.

Blades spoke emphatically about the importance of a general education to back up creative pursuits. He also pointed out that in order to be a good songwriter, one ought to have a real knowledge of music, including the ability to play an instrument. After his initial success, Blades went back to his first music teacher so that he could enhance his talent with an academic understanding of music theory. He wanted to be able to talk easily with other musicians, without worrying that they would disrespect him or think he was a fluke.

During the mid-1980s, Blades finally got the chance to act in a film by a major motion picture studio when he accepted a role in *Critical Condition*, a comedy starring Richard Pryor. Blades played the part of an orderly in a big-city hospital who befriends Pryor's character, a mental patient who pretends to be a doctor during a power failure. The orderly wants to do something better with his life and is discouraged by how the hospital is run. The mental patient, who had made his fantasy become reality, gives the orderly hope of changing his life.

Originally, the orderly was conceived as a white punk, but Paramount reshaped it for Blades, giving the character a Hispanic background. Blades played it as straight as he could. "There already was an all-out comic character—Pryor—and the two of us are constantly getting into ridiculous situations, so I felt no need to clown around," said Blades. "Not that I can't be funny. People think that because some of my songs are about serious issues that I have no sense of humor. On the contrary, it's my sense of humor that keeps me going."

Critical Condition did not turn out to be the success for which Paramount had hoped, but as soon as filming was finished, Blades was already on his way to New Mexico to begin four months of work on his next picture, *The Milagro Beanfield War.* Blades was drawn to this project because it was a far cry from the typical portrayal of Hispanic Americans as people wallowing in poverty, drugs, and crime. Directed by Robert Redford and starring Sonia Braga and

Blades appears with Chick Vennera in a scene from the film The Milagro Beanfield War. *The role of the harried New Mexico sheriff came naturally to Blades, who closely identified with anyone trying to promote understanding between Hispanic and Anglo cultures.*

Christopher Walken, *The Milagro Beanfield War* was the first big-budget Hollywood film to focus on the political conflict between Latins and Anglos. Based on a novel by John Nichols, the film portrays the people of a poor Latin community forced to choose between their culture and land and the promise of Anglo-controlled prosperity.

The Milagro Beanfield War gave Blades an important chance to display his own low-key comedic talents as Sheriff Bernabe Montoya, the somewhat bumbling middleman who tries to calm both the local people and the land developers who are fighting over the future of a small town in New Mexico. According to the movie's producer, Moctesuma Esparza, Blades was selected for the part over 2,000 others because he captured the feeling, the rhythms, and the tempo of the Hispanic personality in the southwestern United States.

Blades was attracted to the character of the slow, deliberate Montoya because he identified with his position as "the man in the middle trying to avoid an explosion, who in the end takes a stand, as we all must." Blades modeled his character after his own father, a policeman in Panama for 24 years. Aware that most Hollywood movies portray Latins by means of a few broad gestures, Blades paid very close attention to the details of Montoya's character. In his direction, Redford told Blades to watch his hands and facial expressions and to imagine that he weighed 250 pounds so that he would move slowly and heavily.

"Most people would think that because these characters are of Mexican origin they must talk like *theees*," Blades later explained. "In fact, they talk like Americans, except with a certain cadence, and a way of rolling the *r*'s that is similar to Costa Ricans. I picked up on the sound right away. After all I'm a musician, so I have a good ear."

When there was a lull in filming, Blades flew back to New York to complete work on his next album, *Agua de Luna* (Moon Water), based on the writings of Gabriel García Márquez. The album had to be recorded in just two weeks to accommodate the film schedule, and the pressure to hurry made Blades very uncomfortable. He wanted above all to do justice to García Márquez's work.

Like Blades's two previous albums, *Agua de Luna* addresses the political, emotional, and moral issues facing the people of Latin America. But unlike *Buscando América* and *Escenas*, which examine the situation in Latin America through contemporary headlines and personal suffering, *Agua de Luna* introduces a broader theme—the need for Latin Americans to overcome their own apathy and assert themselves against domination by foreign interests. "Behind every military coup, behind every civilian dictatorship, lies civilian responsibility," Blades told an interviewer. "We allowed it to happen. We did not look inside, we did not act from within. We voted and then went home."

Although Blades employs some of García Márquez's characters and literary techniques, his songs are not direct adaptations of the writer's work. "The songs don't retell the stories," Blades explained, "but express the emotions I felt reading them." Blades's friendship with García Márquez gave him the freedom to interpret the stories in ways that García Márquez himself had never considered. In "No Te Duermas" (Don't Fall Asleep), which is adapted from the story "Bitterness for Three Sleepwalkers," Blades equated the mysterious illness of a young woman with the unconscious state of Latin America:

> Don't fall asleep, old child;
> don't fall asleep, lying on the patio;
> don't fall asleep, wake up sister.
> Don't fall asleep, I'm watching you.
> I screamed to break up the cage of her torment.
> I screamed to erase the presence of her silence.

"I don't know if Gabriel ever considered the possibility of that story being interpreted as a cry against insanity or a cry against the state of sleepwalking in Latin America today," Blades explained. "In the context of his work, though, I don't think he'll be angry about it."

Gabriel García Márquez, the Nobel Prize-winning Colombian novelist, had been one of Blades's favorite authors since the 1960s. In 1987, Blades realized one of his great ambitions by releasing the album Agua de Luna, *which was based on García Márquez's writings.*

Not only was García Márquez not angry; he was outspoken in support of Blades's use of his material. "I think people thought my stories were going to be sung, and they weren't," said García Márquez. "What Rubén did was to become inspired by my stories. I think the immense majority of Latin Americans are not aware of their problems. But many musicians, many writers, many artists in general are contributing to building that awareness. And Rubén is one of them. If I were a Panamanian, I would vote for him as president of the Republic."

In the spring and fall of 1986, Blades also helped increase awareness of other political problems around the world by taking part in events aimed at raising social consciousness. One such event was the Youth Festival and Anti-Apartheid rally in Dortmund, West Germany, where he appeared along with reggae star Jimmy Cliff. Another was a two-week, six-city tour to benefit the human rights organization Amnesty International. On the Amnesty tour, he appeared with such performing artists as Sting, U2, Peter Gabriel, Jackson Browne, and Peter, Paul and Mary. Still another was the Crack Down concert at Madison Square Garden, held to raise money for the battle against the deadly drug crack (a crystalline form of cocaine): Blades shared the bill with the guitarist Carlos Santana; Crosby, Stills and Nash; Run-DMC; and Felix Cavaliere, among others. On the *Escenas* album, Blades had expressed his feelings about the drug culture in a searing condemnation entitled "Caína" (Caine):

> It stirs and mixes you, the sinner; after it embraces you,
> then it swallows you. You can't love Caine; you can't believe
> in Caine. You think that you have it under control, but with-
> out it, you're nothing. You just can't love Caine; you can not
> trust Caine.

In December 1987, Blades appeared at the Big Blue 2 benefit concert at Madison Square Garden, which raised money for a second New York City Mobile Medical Unit. There he got to live out a dream of his youth by singing the doo-wop classic "Teenager in Love" with Dion; on this occasion, the six Belmonts (Dion's backup group) were Blades, Bruce Springsteen, Lou Reed, Billy Joel, James Taylor, and Paul Simon, the event's host.

In order to meet the dual demands of his film and music careers, Blades decided to rent a small apartment in Los Angeles. The transition was not easy for him. For one thing, he had never learned to drive, and the lack of a car is a serious handicap in a large, spread-out city such as Los Angeles. In addition, he was used to going out and looking for music engagements when he needed them and arranging his own work schedule. In the movie business, he found, it was more customary to sit at home and wait for the phone to ring.

Fortunately, Blades's work in *The Milagro Beanfield War*— released in the fall of 1987 without much critical or financial success—had won the praise of critics, many of whom rated his performance the most enjoyable part of the film. A number of producers expressed interest in signing Blades up for other films. When the roles came, however, the final result was not under

Blades's control the way a concert or a record album was. When he costarred with comedian Whoopi Goldberg in *Fatal Beauty*, the film earned poor reviews and failed at the box office. This formula was repeated several times during Blades's developing film career: Critics and audiences appreciated his work, but the films themselves were quickly forgotten.

Blades attends a New York film premiere with his wife, the actress Lisa Lebenzon, in 1990. Blades's Hollywood acting career and his marriage to the blonde, blue-eyed Lebenzon drew fire from his critics in the Latin community, but he staunchly defended his freedom of choice.

When the album *Agua de Luna* was released in January 1988, Blades won increasing recognition from the mainstream press and the entertainment industry. He began to appear on a variety of popular television programs, ranging from Johnny Carson's "Tonight Show" to "Sesame Street" and "60 Minutes." Blades's appearances in Europe had also created a following for him there, and British filmmakers featured him in a video entitled *The Return of Rubén Blades.*

While he was enjoying this recognition, Blades was often compelled to defend the integrity of his work and his Latin identity. There were those in the Latin community who accused him of selling out, first for his 1987 move to Los Angeles and then for his marriage to a blonde, blue-eyed American actress, Lisa Lebenzon, in the same year. Blades dismissed these objections in an interview with David Fricke of *Rolling Stone:* "Because I make a movie with Redford, does that mean I can't go to El Corso [a Latin dance hall in Manhattan], that I'm dealing with my musicians differently? If I bump into a guy in the street and he says 'Qué pasa, Rubén?' does that mean I don't say 'Qué pasa?' back? Do I turn my back? I don't do that."

Replying to other critics who felt that he was trying to do too many things at once, Blades said, "One of the things I've done in my life is to move in as many directions as I feel my talent can take me. I'm not going to become limited to 'this is what you're gonna do, this is it.' I know that has created confusion for those who market talent, but I'd rather do that than become the flavor of the month, and then be dismissed for the next flavor."

Blades performs at the Playboy Jazz Festival in Los Angeles in 1989. Eager to convey his message to non-Latin audiences, Blades made a habit of explaining his songs in English during concerts and providing translations in the liner notes of his albums.

CHAPTER EIGHT

Nothing But the Truth

Four months before Blades's 40th birthday, Elektra released his new album, *Nothing But the Truth.* The album marked Blades's first in-depth collaboration with such non-Latin artists as the former leader of the Velvet Underground, Lou Reed, and the British rocker Elvis Costello. It was also the first album Blades had recorded entirely in English. He had long considered the possibility of making this switch; in fact, his contract with Elektra called for English-language productions.

Blades realized that the album was another opportunity to break down the barriers between Hispanic and Anglo cultures. "I want people to acknowledge the possibilities of Latin artists fully— meaning we can do English, too," he said. "We were raised with rock and roll. We were raised with the U.S. culture banging in our heads. I think people in the States don't know that. In general they think we don't have any understanding of the culture. And the only way we can change that is to sing in their own language."

By 1988, Blades was no longer so alone in his desire to reach English-speaking audiences. At the time *Nothing But the Truth* was released, Hispanic influences on American culture—film, theater, music, design, dance, and art—were being felt as never before. Between 1980 and 1988, the Hispanic population in the United States had grown by 30 percent, and the Hispanic influence on all areas of mainstream American life was increasing. This trend was represented by such films as *La Bamba, Stand and Deliver,* and *Salsa* as well as the emergence of actors such as Edward James Olmos, Andy Garcia, and Maria Conchita Alonso. In the recording industry, new artists were introducing the Latin sound into mainstream rock music: Los Lobos, Lisa Lisa and Cult Jam, and the Miami Sound Machine were appealing to audiences eager for the rhythms of the Caribbean and Latin America.

Much of the material on *Nothing But the Truth* explores the connection between love and violence. According to Blades, violence is born of the inability to resolve problems in other ways; violence is love gone crazy. His collaborations with Costello on such songs as "The Miranda Syndrome" and "Shamed into Love" and with Reed on "Hopes on Hold" were lengthy, soul-searching sessions.

Blades was not ashamed to admit that he had enlisted Lou Reed and Elvis Costello because he was afraid he could not write well enough in English; he attributed this fear to what he called his "Latin American inferiority complex," an interesting statement from one who speaks fluent English and holds a degree from Harvard. Blades overcame his uncertainty by thinking out the lyrics in Spanish; then he wrote them down in English, relying on Reed and Costello to tell him how the words worked with the music.

Nothing But the Truth did not shy away from Blades's usual political concerns in order to pursue a more general pop appeal. The album tackled some of the major issues of its day, such as Oliver North's involvement in the Iran-contra scandal ("Ollie's Doo-Wop") and the emergence of the AIDS crisis ("The Letter").

In "Salvador," Blades proved that he had not abandoned his passionate concern for the fate of Latin America:

> In Salvador
> Women come out
> To show the moon
> Our heads covered with blood.

"There are 11 different styles of songs on this record," he said. "I wanted to present a whole fabric of different colors and sounds and put them together on a record the way I remembered radio to be when radio played all different kinds of music." Although it impressed the critics and made several top 10 lists, *Nothing But the Truth* was not a commercial success. Blades was not discouraged by the sales figures: He believed that the album would have a long life because people would return to it again and again over the years.

As if anticipating the inevitable charge that he was turning his back on his Latin audience, Blades began recording his next album, *Antecedente* (Heritage), even before *Nothing But the Truth* was released. Recorded in Spanish with Blades's new band, Son del Solar (Sound of the Tenement)—which included some of the musicians from his previous group—*Antecedente* reincorporates the trombones Blades had cut out after breaking with Willie Colón years before. More significant, the album celebrates the sights and sounds of Latin America and explores Blades's childhood memories. Most of the songs bear the mark of Blades's keen awareness of life's difficulties—lost loves, old friends on the wrong side of the law, an Indian selling black-market goods deep in the jungles of the Orinoco—but "Plaza Herrera" shows Blades in a mood of deep nostalgia:

> Herrera Plaza, small park
> where in the afternoons
> a tired sun rests.
> On your benches I dreamt on
> while my young hopes were painted blue by the moon.

Old neighborhood that brings to me
sweet memories of a childhood long gone.
Herrera Plaza, I still remember you because
you never erased my footsteps,
because you still keep in you
those hours when, as a child, I loved.

Despite his nostalgia for Panama, Blades was spending more and more time in Los Angeles and had recently completed one of his most challenging roles in *Dead Man Out*, a made-for-cable film in which he portrays a convict on death row who has gone insane while in prison. Danny Glover plays the psychiatrist who tries to restore his sanity; according to the law, the authorities will not be able to execute him until he is declared sane.

Blades relished the emotionally complex role and particularly appreciated the purpose of the movie, which examines the important issue of prison violence and the contradictions of capital punishment. "We still haven't resolved the question of what jails are for," he explained. "Are we punishing people? Rehabilitating people? Merely taking them out of circulation? For me, until that question gets resolved, killing people just perpetuates not only the question but the absurdity."

The role of the Jewish gangster Mickey Nice in The Two Jakes *gave Blades a chance to play a non-Latin character. Jack Nicholson, the film's star and director, said that Blades "brought a lot of energy and good acting instincts to the role."*

The film was shot mostly in a prison in the Province of Quebec, Canada, and the experience reminded Blades of the work he had done with prisoners when he was a student in Panama, researching the effects of prison conditions. "This drama was a way of bringing out a voice that I found that time in jail that had not been given a chance to express itself before," he said. "As an attorney, I've learned that most people think they'll never be in jail. Most people think, 'I'm a good person. I go to church. I have a job.' But anyone can end up in jail. Somebody drinks, runs over someone. All of a sudden there you are."

For his performance in *Dead Man Out*, Blades received an ACE Award for best actor in a made-for-cable film and was offered a string of other film roles. Within the next two years, he appeared alongside such notable actors as Diane Keaton in *The Lemon Sisters*, Jack Nicholson in *The Two Jakes*, Denzel Washington in *Mo' Better Blues*, Anthony Hopkins in the HBO special *One Man's War*, Joe Pesci in *The Super*, and Danny Glover again in *Predator 2*. He also did another cable TV special, playing the manager and lover of dancer Josephine Baker in *The Josephine Baker Story*, and earned an Emmy nomination for his performance.

A scene from the 1990 film Mo' Better Blues, *in which Blades plays a nervous bookie opposite Spike Lee, who also produced, wrote, and directed the film. Lee is one of the many filmmakers and critics who appreciates Blades's low-key, seemingly effortless acting style.*

The Two Jakes was especially noteworthy because it allowed Blades to expand his range; in the film, set in Los Angeles during the late 1940s, he plays Mickey Nice, a Jewish gangster. Filmmaker Spike Lee, who cast Blades as a nervous bookie in *Mo' Better Blues*, summed up his appeal: "He is a very naturalistic actor. I look for people who are natural in front of the camera."

Although Blades once claimed that he acts in order to support his music, all his efforts—in film, music, writing, and law—increasingly underscored his determination to begin a political career in Panama. Throughout the 1980s, Blades watched with dismay as General Manuel Noriega consolidated his power and pocketed immense wealth at the expense of the Panamanian people. Because the dictator was willing to let the United States use Panama as a base for secret operations against the left-wing regime in Nicaragua, officials in Washington turned a blind eye to Noriega's increasingly brutal, repressive rule and his flourishing international drug trade.

By 1987, Noriega's violent tactics had alienated Panama's powerful banking community. (Panama's banking laws place fewer restrictions on banks than do the laws of most other nations; as a result, Panama has become a major center of financial activity, both legitimate and otherwise.) To show their displeasure with Noriega, the bankers withheld more than $1 billion from the country's already weak economy. When Noriega desperately turned to the Soviet Union, Cuba, and other Communist-led governments for help, U.S. president George Bush decided that he was no longer a suitable ally and suggested that he resign. Noriega refused. The U.S. government then indicted him on drug charges, imposed economic sanctions on Panama, and instigated a coup by army officers, all of which failed to oust Noriega from power. Finally, in December 1989, the U.S. Army invaded Panama, captured Noriega, and brought him to the United States. As of 1991, he remained in a Florida jail, awaiting trial on drug charges.

Although he despised Noriega, Blades denounced the U.S. invasion of Panama as a "flagrant transgression of international law." He spoke about founding an independent political party that could speak for Panamanians who are not represented either by Noriega's party or by the U.S.-backed government of President Guillermo Endara.

Even with Noriega gone, Panama's problems continued— crime, poverty, economic chaos, internal political feuds, drug trafficking, and continued domination by the United States. Blades had a very different vision of his homeland's future. "What I propose is to create what up to this point has been a mythical place," he said, "a Latin America that respects and loves itself, is incorruptible, romantic, nationalistic and has a perception of the needs of the world at large." In the song "Prohibido Olvidar" (It Is Prohibited to Forget), which condemns the abuses of Latin American dictatorship, he stated this ideal in down-to-earth terms: "Each nation depends on the heart / of its people, / and a country which doesn't sell out / can't be bought by anybody."

"Prohibido Olvidar" was featured on the album *Caminando* (Walking), released in early 1991. As on *Antecedente*, all the songs on the new album were sung in Spanish, with Blades's English translations included in the liner notes. This time, however, the accent was

The Chorillo district of Panama City lay in ruins in December 1989 after U.S. troops invaded the country in order to depose General Manuel Antonio Noriega. Blades detested Noriega, but he condemned the U.S. action as "a flagrant transgression of international law."

not entirely on Latin American themes; returning to his earlier approach, Blades chose to pursue a wide range of subjects, both personal and political. The title song of the album is a pure celebration of life, from the point of view of one who is always seeking new experiences: "Walking, is how one learns in life. / Walking, is how you know what it is. / Walking, the wound is cured. / Walking, you leave yesterday behind." The following song, "Camaleón" (Chameleon), condemns a false friend; "Ella Se Esconde" (She Hides) laments a love gone sour; "Obalue" pays tribute to the folk religions of the Caribbean; and "El" (He) tells the story of a friend who is unsure of his sexual identity.

However much ground he covered, though, Blades always returned to the struggle of life. In "Mientras Duerme la Ciudad" (While the City Sleeps), he etches a biting view of a society in which everyone scrambles to get a slice of the pie:

> At night
> The upper class conspires
> highball in hand
> planning schemes
> The middle class rests
> maimed
> watching television
> The lower class goes on, way below
> Waiting for the day in which changes will come
> Night arrives, covering us all with its shawl
> Some wrap themselves with lies
> Others cover themselves with truth
> The entire world bets on life
> While the city sleeps.

When discussing his plans for the rest of the 1990s, Blades emphasized his determination to keep on breaking new ground. "I will never be a superstar," he told Guy D. Garcia in *Time* magazine. "My role is to be different, to do what others won't do, and, as a result, my fortunes will always fluctuate. I will always be viewed with suspicion by some, though not by all, because I move against the current."

Although his singing and acting careers continue to flourish, Blades has often stated his intention to enter politics in Panama during the 1990s. "I can't sing forever with the world exploding around me," he has declared.

Blades's determination to have an impact on the political life of Panama remains strong, and he has vowed on many occasions that he will return to his homeland permanently before the end of the decade. "My life is a cycle that began in Panama, and it will close there," he declared. He did not discuss the effect of such a move on his music and film careers, other than to say, "Emotionally, nothing beats the music." The final cut on *Caminando*, "Raíz de Sueños" (Root of Dreams), suggests that whatever decision Blades makes about his future, he will hold fast to his heritage and his hopes for the future of Latin America:

> My Caribbean basin root of dreams
> Where feelings never tire.
> I am from the land of hope.
> I have the blood of those who are
> not subject to ownership.
> I am like fire and moon,
> Water and memory,
> Ever lit dawns, always illuminating
> Our history.

Selected Discography and Filmography

<u>Albums</u>

1977   Willie Colón and Rubén Blades: *Metiendo Mano*
Fania Records

1978   Willie Colón and Rubén Blades: *Siembra*
Fania Records

1980   Rubén Blades: *Maestra Vida: Primera Parte*
Fania Records

1980   Rubén Blades: *Maestra Vida: Segunda Parte*
Fania Records

1981   Willie Colón and Rubén Blades: *Canciones del Solar de los Aburridos*
Fania Records

1983   Rubén Blades: *Greatest Hits*
Musica Latina International, Inc.

1984   Rubén Blades: *Mucho Mejor*
Fania Records

1984   Rubén Blades y Seis del Solar: *Buscando América*
Elektra/Asylum

1985   Rubén Blades y Seis del Solar: *Escenas*
Elektra/Asylum

1987   Rubén Blades y Seis del Solar: *Agua de Luna*
Elektra/Asylum

1988   Rubén Blades: *Nothing But the Truth*
Elektra/Asylum

1988   Rubén Blades y Son del Solar: *Antecedente*
Elektra/Asylum

1990   Rubén Blades y Son del Solar: *Live*
Elektra/Asylum

1991   Rubén Blades con Son del Solar: *Caminando*
Sony Discos

Films

1981   *The Last Fight*
1985   *Crossover Dreams*
1986   *Critical Condition*
1987   *The Milagro Beanfield War*
1988   *Fatal Beauty*
1990   *Dead Man Out*
1990   *Predator 2*
1990   *The Lemon Sisters*
1990   *Mo' Better Blues*
1990   *The Two Jakes*
1991   *The Josephine Baker Story*
1991   *One Man's War*
1991   *The Super*

Chronology

July 16, 1948	Born Rubén Blades in Panama City, Panama
1964	Panamanians clash with U.S. troops in the Panama Canal Zone
1968	Blades enrolls in University of Panama
1969	After the university is shut down due to political unrest, Blades visits New York City and performs with Pete Rodríguez
1972	Graduates with a degree in law from the University of Panama and begins working for the Banco Nacional de Panamá
1974	Moves to New York City and debuts at Madison Square Garden with Ray Barretto
1976	Signs with Fania Records and forms musical partnership with Willie Colón
1978	Colón and Blades's album *Siembra* is released
1981	General Manuel Noriega becomes the dictator of Panama
1982	Blades breaks with Colón and forms his own group, Seis del Solar

1984	Signs with Elektra/Asylum, which releases *Buscando América*; "Decisiones" is banned in Panama
1985	Blades earns master's degree in international law from Harvard University; *Crossover Dreams* opens; *Escenas* is released; Blades performs at Carnegie Hall
1987	Moves to Los Angeles and marries Lisa Lebenzon; wins Grammy Award for *Escenas*; appears in "Sun City" video; *The Milagro Beanfield War* opens; *Agua de Luna* is released
1988	Collaborates with Lou Reed and Elvis Costello on English-language album, *Nothing But the Truth*
1989	*Antecedente* is released; Noriega ousted as dictator of Panama
1990	Blades wins ACE Award for *Dead Man Out*
1991	*Caminando* is released; Blades nominated for Emmy Award; announces plans to run for political office in Panama

Further Reading

Barol, Bill. "Salsa with a Political Spin." *Newsweek* (September 9, 1985).

Cocks, Jay. "The Keen Edge of Rubén Blades." *Time* (July 2, 1984).

DePalma, Anthony. "Ruben Blades: Up from Salsa." *New York Times Magazine* (June 21, 1987).

Fernandez, Enrique. "Ruben Blades: Crossover Dreaming." *Elle* (January, 1987).

Fricke, David. "Ruben Blades's Latin Revolution." *Rolling Stone* (April 23, 1987).

Garcia, Guy D. "Singer, Actor, Politico." *Time* (January 29, 1990).

Gerard, Charley, and Marty Sheller. *Salsa! The Rhythm of Latin Music.* Indiana: White Cliffs Media, 1989.

Hamill, Pete. "Hey, It's Rubén Blades: A Latin Star Makes His Move." *New York* (August 19, 1985).

————. "It's Rubén's Time!" *ASCAP in Action* (Spring 1986).

Holden, Stephen. "Rubén Blades Turns His Talents to Movies." *New York Times* (August 18, 1985).

LaFeber, Walter. *The Panama Canal: The Crisis in Historical Perspective.* New York: Oxford University Press, 1989.

"More Than a Question of Flags." *Newsweek* (January 20, 1964).

"Who Really Owns Panama: A Source of U.S. Trouble." *U.S. News & World Report* (April 6, 1964).

Index

Afro-Cuban music, 34, 38, 60
Agua de Luna, 86–87, 91
Amnesty International, 88
Antecedente, 95, 99
Arce, Manuel, 71, 72, 74
Arias, Arnulfo, 33–34, 35
Artists United Against Apartheid, 82
Balboa High School, 18, 21
Barretto, Ray, 39, 46, 47, 48
Beatles, 16, 29
Beat Street, 67
Berry, Chuck, 16
Big Blue 2 benefit, 89
Blades, Anoland (mother), 25,28–
    29, 30, 36
Blades, Luis (brother), 30, 37
Blades, Rubén
    birth, 25
    childhood, 26–28
    film career, 70–75, 84–86, 89–
      90, 96–98
    law career, 41, 43
    musical influences, 16–17, 21,
      27–29
    music career, 30, 31, 37, 39, 41,
      45, 47–52, 55–61, 66, 67, 79,
      81–82, 86–87, 89, 91, 93, 94
    political involvement, 31, 34–
      36, 62, 82, 88–89, 98–99, 101
    receives ACE Award, 97
    receives Grammy Award, 76
    songwriting career, 44, 48–49,
      50–51, 53, 62–66, 76–79, 84,
      87–88, 94–96, 99–100, 101
    teenage years, 15–17, 21, 23,
      28–31
    university studies, 34–37, 41,
      67, 69–70, 75
Blades, Rubén, Sr. (father), 25, 28
Bono, 82
Bosques Laurenza, Emma
    (grandmother), 25–26, 30, 70
Braga, Sonia, 85
Brecht, Bertolt, 44, 49
Buscando América, 60, 62, 66, 67, 73,
    74, 76, 87
Bush and the Magnificos, 34
"Caína," 89
Cambridge, Massachusetts, 67, 69,
    70
Caminando, 99, 101
Canby, Vincent, 74
"Canción del Final del Mundo, La,"
    76, 82
Canciones de Mi Padre (Ronstadt),
    78–79
Cannes Film Festival, 66
Carlson, Lisa, 69
Carnegie Hall, 79, 81, 82
Cavaliere, Felix, 89

Central Intelligence Agency, U.S., 61
Cliff, Jimmy, 88
Cocks, Jay, 60
Colón, Willie, 39, 46, 48, 50, 52, 53, 55, 70, 95
Costello, Elvis, 93
Crack Down concert, 89
Cristal, Pancho, 34, 41
Critical Condition, 84, 85
Crossover Dreams, 70, 72, 73, 74
Cuba, Joe, 31, 34, 37, 41
Cuba, 25, 38, 50, 51, 98
Dead Man Out, 96, 97
"Decisiones," 66, 82
De Panamá a Nueva York, 41
"Desapariciones," 64–65
Dion, 89
Dylan, Bob, 44, 57, 82
Elektra/Asylum Records, 57, 60, 73, 76, 93
"Ella Se Esconde," 100
Endara, Guillermo, 99
Escenas, 76–78, 79, 87
Esparza, Moctesuma, 86
Estrella de Panamá, 52
Fania All-Stars, 47
Fania Records, 45, 47, 48, 50, 53, 56, 70
Fatal Beauty, 90
Fricke, David, 91
Garcia, Guy D., 100
García Márquez, Gabriel, 53, 67, 86, 87, 88
Gerard, Charley, 38, 61
Glover, Danny, 96
Gómez, Tito, 47
Gorgas, William C., 19
Grammy Awards, 60, 76, 78
Guarare, 48
Haley, Bill, 16
Hamill, Pete, 79
Harvard University, 35, 67, 69, 70, 74, 75, 82

Hernández, Oscar, 55
"Hopes on Hold," 94
Hopkins, Anthony, 97
Ichaso, Leon, 71, 72, 73–74
Irizarry, Ralph, 55
Jackson, Joe, 76
Josephine Baker Story, The, 97
Keaton, Diane, 97
Last Fight, The, 70, 71
LaVoe, Hector, 39, 48
Lebenzon, Lisa, 91
Lecuona, Ernesto, 25
Lee, Spike, 98
Los Angeles, California, 52, 89, 91, 96, 98
Los Lobos, 94
Lymon, Frankie, 16, 28
Machito, 39
Madison Square Garden, 47, 79, 88, 89
Maestra Vida, 53
Marrero, Ricardo, 55, 56
Masucci, Jerry, 48, 70
Max Mambru Films, 71, 72
Metiendo Mano, 48
Miami, Florida, 51, 52
"Mientras Duerme la Ciudad," 100
Milagro Beanfield War, The, 85–86, 89
Mo' Better Blues, 97, 98
Montreux International Jazz Festival, 66
Moré, Beny, 27, 28
"Muévete," 76
National Guard, 34, 36, 41, 61
New York City, 16, 29, 37, 38, 39, 41, 43, 44, 45–46, 50, 52, 63, 66, 69, 72, 74, 79, 86, 89
New York magazine, 79
New York Times, 40, 60, 74, 82
Nichols, John, 86
Nicholson, Jack, 97
Noriega, Manuel Antonio, 61, 98, 99

North, Oliver, 94
Nothing But the Truth, 93, 94–95
One Man's War, 97
Orquesta Casino de la Playa, 27
Pacheco, Johnny, 39, 46
"Padre Antonio y el Monaguillo Andrés, El," 63–64, 65–66
Palmer, Robert, 60
Panama, University of, 15, 34, 37, 43
Panama Canal Zone, 15, 17–18, 19–20, 21, 22, 29, 61
Panama City, 15, 20, 22, 25
Pareles, Jon, 82
Parker, Charlie, 39
Paxton, Tom, 44
"Pedro Navaja," 49
Pesci, Joe, 97
Piero, 31, 44
"Plata Herrera," 95–96
Presley, Elvis, 16, 29
Pryor, Richard, 84, 85
Puente, Tito, 39
Redford, Robert, 85, 86, 91
Reed, Lou, 82, 89, 93, 94
Return of Rubén Blades, The, 91
Rivera, Louie, 55
Robles, Marco A., 33, 34
Rock and roll, 16, 17, 21, 23, 28, 30, 31, 55, 61, 82, 93
Rock, Rock, Rock, 16
Rock Around the Clock, 16
Rodríguez, Bobby, 48
Rodríguez, Pete, 41
Rolling Stone magazine, 60, 72, 91
Romero, Oscar Arnulfo, 62
Ronstadt, Linda, 76, 77, 78
Roosevelt, Theodore, 19, 25
Sabournin, Tony, 38, 39

Salsa, 38, 39, 40, 45, 47, 48, 49, 50, 53, 55, 56, 60, 70, 71, 76, 81
Salsa! The Rhythm of Latin Music (Gerard and Sheller), 38
"Salvador," 95
Santana, Carlos, 89
"Saturday Night Live," 71
Seeger, Pete, 44
Seis del Solar, 55, 66, 67, 82
"Sesame Street," 91
Sheller, Marty, 38, 61
Siembra, 48, 50, 56, 70
Simon, Paul, 89
Sinatra, Frank, 30, 49
Soler, Octavio, 71
Son del Solar, 95
Springsteen, Bruce, 82, 83, 89
"Sun City," 82
Super, The, 97
Threepenny Opera, The, 44
"Tiburón," 50–52
"Tierra Dura," 77
Time magazine, 60, 100
Tormé, Mel, 27
Torrijos Herrera, Omar, 36–37, 61
Two Jakes, The, 97, 98
United Nations, 43
U.S. Army, 19, 98
U.S. Panama Canal Company, 19
Van Zandt, Steve, 82
Village Gate, 79, 81
Village Voice, 34, 60
Vincent, Gene, 29
Viñas, Mike, 55
Walken, Christopher, 86
Washington, Denzel, 97
Weill, Kurt, 44, 49
Williamson, Fred "the Hammer," 70

BETTY A. MARTON has been working as a writer since 1981, when she graduated from Columbia University's Graduate School of Journalism. Her articles have appeared in many consumer and professional publications. She has taught writing at Manhattan College and currently lives with her husband and young son in New York City.

RODOLFO CARDONA is professor of Spanish and comparative literature at Boston University. A renowned scholar, he has written many works of criticism, including *Ramón, a Study of Gómez de la Serna and His Works* and *Visión del esperpento: Teoría y práctica del esperpento en Valle-Inclán*. Born in San José, Costa Rica, he earned his B.A. and M.A. from Louisiana State University and received a Ph.D. from the University of Washington. He has taught at Case Western Reserve University, the University of Pittsburgh, the University of Texas at Austin, the University of New Mexico, and Harvard University.

JAMES COCKCROFT is currently a visiting professor of Latin American and Caribbean studies at the State University of New York at Albany. A three-time Fulbright scholar, he earned a Ph.D. from Stanford University and has taught at the University of Massachusetts, the University of Vermont, and the University of Connecticut. He is the author or coauthor of numerous books on Latin American subjects, including *Neighbors in Turmoil: Latin America*, *The Hispanic Experience in the United States: Contemporary Issues and Perspectives*, and *Outlaws in the Promised Land: Mexican Immigrant Workers and America's Future*.

PICTURE CREDITS

AP/Wide World Photos: pp. 17, 20, 24, 62; Randy Bauer/Ron Galella, Ltd.: p. 90; Photo by Ricardo Betancourt: p. 54; The Bettmann Archive: p. 29; Frank Driggs Collection: pp. 32, 37, 39, 40, 92; Photo by Paul Kirchner: p. 71; Courtesy of Max Mambru Films: pp. 68, 76; Courtesy of Max Mambru Films, photo by Octavio Soler: p. 73; The Museum of Modern Art/Film Stills Archive: pp. 85, 96, 97; The Music Division, The New York Public Library/Astor, Lenox and Tilden Foundations: p. 27; Gilles Peress/Magnum Photos: p. 83; Reuters/Bettmann Archive: pp. 88, 99; Photo by Heriberto Rios: p. 42; Courtesy of Sonido, Inc.: pp. 46, 49, 52; Courtesy of Sony Records and *FAMA* magazine: pp. 14, 101; Courtesy of Juan Toro: pp. 56, 81; UPI/Bettmann Archive: pp. 22, 30, 35, 44, 57, 63, 65, 78

All lyrics © Rubén Blades Productions Inc., May 1984, 1986, 1987, 1988, 1991. Used by permission.